Sacred Chaos — Devotional for Moms

WEEKLY CHRISTIAN INSPIRATION TO NURTURE SPIRITUAL RENEWAL, PEACE, AND PURPOSE IN THE WHIRLWIND OF MOTHERHOOD

DAVID & MARY BETH NELSON

Contents

Welcome!

MOTHERHOOD IS BEAUTIFUL, EXHAUSTING, JOYFUL, overwhelming, sacred, and messy—all at the same time.

Some days, you feel like you're thriving. Other days, you wonder if you're even getting the basics right. There are moments when love flows easily, and moments when patience feels like an impossible ask. Through it all, there's one constant: you are not alone.

This book is here to remind you of that—again and again.

In fact, you might notice that message echoing through many of these pages. It may feel repetitive at times, but that's by design. Some truths are worth planting deep, so they can take root in the moments you need them most.

How to Use This Devotional: You'll see a "Week #" at the top of each entry, but here's the secret: that number isn't a rule—it's just a gentle guide. This book isn't a rigid plan or a spiritual checklist. It's an invitation.

The devotionals are grouped into six themed sections, but you can read them in any order. Go week by week, or skip around. Some entries will meet you right in the thick of what you're facing; others may speak to a season you've already walked or haven't reached yet. All of it is here for you—when you need it.

However you move through these pages, know this: there's no "right way." This is not homework. This is your oasis.

No Pressure, Just Grace: If you're reading this while reheating your coffee for the third time, hiding in the bathroom for a moment of silence, or stealing a few quiet minutes before everyone wakes up— you belong here. This space is for you.

These entries aren't about fixing anything or becoming a perfect mom (spoiler: there's no such thing). They're about finding God in your real, messy, beautiful life—in the dishes, the tantrums, the errands, the late-night worries, and the unexpected giggles.

God isn't waiting for you to have it all together before He shows up. He's already here.

An Invitation to Exhale: At the end of each devotional, you'll find a short section called *Weave it into Your Day*—simple suggestions for reflection or action. Some may already be part of your routine. Others might stretch your faith muscles a bit. None are time-sensitive or pressure-filled. Use them however they serve you.

Though this book carries both of our names, Mary Beth did most of the writing, pouring her heart and lived experience into these pages. David served as editor, encourager, and sounding board every step of the way. This is our shared offering—but one born especially from a mother's heart to yours.

Take a breath. Open to the page that calls to you. Let these words remind you that your work matters, your love is seen, and even on the hardest days, you are still sacred. Still growing. Still held by a God who never stops loving you.

Welcome to *Sacred Chaos*. This is holy ground.

With love,

David & Mary Beth

PART ONE

The Beautiful Mess

Motherhood is not neat. It's cluttered with mismatched socks, endless snack crumbs, and the ever-growing to-do list. It's made up of repetitive routines—dishes, laundry, school drop-offs, bedtime battles—that can feel more like survival than something sacred.

But what if holiness is hidden in the mess?

What if God is just as present in the folding of onesies as He is in the quiet of a church pew? What if the exhausting work of mothering is not just something to endure but something that *transforms* us?

This section is about meeting God in the ordinary—learning to see your home as **holy ground**, where love is lived out in small, unseen acts. He is here, right now, in the middle of your messy, beautiful life. And He is speaking—even through the hum of the washing machine, the late-night lullabies, and the scattered toys underfoot.

This is the beautiful mess. And it is sacred.

Week 1

WHEN THE DISHES PREACH

SCRIPTURE

"So whether you eat or drink or whatever you do, do it all for the glory of God."

— 1 Corinthians 10:31 (NIV)

Devotional

You didn't sign up for a sermon at the sink. But somehow, as you stare at the mountain of dishes, the lesson starts to rise up — one cup, one plate, one fork at a time. It's not profound. It's not pretty. It's just the next thing.

This is your life right now. Sticky counters. Forgotten lunches. Fifteen minutes of cleaning just to make it look like nothing exploded. The dishwasher's full. The sink is still full. And somehow, the cereal bowls have multiplied again. There's nothing glamorous about this moment. But that doesn't mean it's meaningless.

Motherhood has a way of burying your effort in repetition. You do so much, and it rarely feels like enough — or like anyone sees. But there's something deeply sacred about the small, faithful things. When done with love, even dishwashing becomes worship. God doesn't measure significance the way we do. He sees what's done in secret, and He values faithfulness over flash.

Jesus didn't avoid the mess. He didn't save His love for mountaintop moments or miracles. He knelt and washed His disciples' dirty feet — one of the lowliest tasks of the time. He didn't just serve; He made service beautiful. And He invited us to do the same.

What if we started to see these ordinary routines — the cleaning, the folding, the driving — as holy ground? What if your kitchen became a sanctuary, your hands instruments of ministry, your daily rhythms a quiet offering?

You are not "just" doing chores. You are building a place where love lives. Every small act is a seed planted in the soil of faith. You may not see the harvest today, but it's growing — in your home, in your kids, in you.

And yes, some days it will feel mindless or endless. But even then, it matters. God meets you in the dishes. He strengthens you in the routine. He honors your unseen sacrifices and uses them to shape hearts — including your own.

So let the dishes preach. Let them remind you that God is present — not just in quiet devotionals or church pews, but right here in the chaos, in the crumbs, and in the clutter. The work is hard. The reward is often invisible. But the glory is His — even here.

Prayer

Lord, help me see the holiness in the ordinary. Remind me that my quiet work is not wasted. Give me joy in the small things and peace in the repetition. Help me honor You, even in the dishes. Amen.

Weave It Into Your Day

As you wash dishes this week, whisper a prayer. Let each plate become a reminder: God is with me in this.

Week 2

GRACE, NOT PERFECTION

SCRIPTURE

"But he said to me, 'My grace is sufficient for you, for my power is made perfect in weakness.' Therefore I will boast all the more gladly about my weaknesses, so that Christ's power may rest on me."

— 2 Corinthians 12:9 (NIV)

Devotional

You had plans for today — good ones. You were going to be calm, patient, and present. The house would stay mostly clean, no one would cry in the car, and maybe—just maybe—you'd get through the day without raising your voice.

And then... real life happened.

The toddler melted down over the wrong color spoon. The big kid forgot their project until five minutes before school. Someone spilled juice on the clean clothes. The to-do list got longer, not shorter. And you? You lost your cool. Again.

And now the guilt creeps in. You wonder, *Why can't I just get it together? Why does everyone else seem to do this better than me?*

Here's the truth: perfection is a lie. And motherhood is not a performance. It's not about being flawless. It's about showing up, again and again, leaning into God's grace in your weakness. His grace doesn't meet you once you've "figured it all out." It meets you in the mess — the exact place where you feel like you're failing.

You don't have to be the perfect mom. You just need to be a *grace-filled* one. Your kids don't need a version of you who never messes up. They need a mom who knows how to apologize, who models humility, who turns back to God when she stumbles.

Perfection demands silence. It tells you to hide your struggle. But grace invites honesty. It says, *Bring your mess to Me. I'm not surprised by it.*

The pressure to be "enough" fades when you remember that Christ is more than enough. His power shows up strongest in our weakest moments. So instead of beating yourself up for not being perfect, what if you asked God to make something beautiful out of your broken places?

Your child won't remember whether the house was spotless or dinner was Pinterest-worthy. But they will remember whether you looked them in the eyes. Whether you spoke life when they messed up. Whether you gave yourself the same grace you want them to know.

You're not failing. You're human. And grace is the gift that reminds you — God's got this. He's not looking for perfection. He's looking for your heart.

Prayer

Father, I'm tired of chasing perfection. Help me receive Your grace when I mess up and to give that same grace to my children. Remind me that You are strong where I am weak. Thank You for loving me through every imperfect moment. Amen.

Weave It Into Your Day

Whenever you mess up this week, stop and whisper, "Grace, not perfection." Let it be your reset button, not your shame trigger.

Week 3

HOLY GROUND IN THE PLAYROOM

SCRIPTURE

"When Jacob awoke from his sleep, he thought, 'Surely the Lord is in this place, and I was not aware of it.'"

— Genesis 28:16 (NIV)

Devotional

The toys are everywhere. There's a doll wedged under the couch, a puzzle missing two pieces, and a LEGO you stepped on five minutes ago that still has your foot throbbing. This room was clean yesterday — maybe even this morning — but now it looks like a toy store exploded. Again.

And in the middle of it all is a tiny voice: "Will you play with me?"

You want to say yes. You also want to clean up, finish the dishes, answer the emails, and fold the laundry. There's never enough time. Never enough you. The mental tug-of-war is exhausting — choosing between the to-do list and the moment in front of you.

But what if the moment in front of you is holy?

Jacob in the Old Testament didn't realize he was on holy ground until after the moment passed. "Surely the Lord is in this place," he said, "and I was not aware of it." That line hits differently when you're in a room full of mismatched toy parts, sticky floors, and a child asking for your attention.

You might not feel spiritual sitting cross-legged next to a pile of action figures or sipping pretend tea from a plastic cup. But God doesn't only meet you in candlelit quiet time or Sunday morning worship. He meets you in the real, loud, everyday stuff of your life — including that moment when you sit down and play.

The playroom — or whatever space your child claims as their own — can become a place of connection, not just between you and them, but between you and God. When you stoop down to their level, when you say yes to presence over productivity, when you laugh or listen or build something small with little hands — that's love in action. That's ministry. That's worship in its most honest form.

You are not wasting your time. You are investing it — planting seeds of security, joy, and trust in your child's heart. In those simple moments, you show them what love looks like when it's quiet and close. And perhaps just as importantly, you remind yourself that you are still part of something sacred — even when it's messy.

Let the playroom be holy ground. Not because it's clean. Not because you have everything under control. But because God is there, working in and through you as you show up with your imperfect, tired, open-hearted self.

Prayer

Lord, help me to recognize You in the ordinary, even in the mess. Give me the wisdom to slow down, the courage to be present, and the joy to meet my child where they are. Let my home — even the messy corners — be holy ground. Amen.

Weave It Into Your Day

Pause this week in one of your child's favorite spaces. Whisper, "God is here, too." Let that truth soften your heart.

Week 4

WHAT IF I'M NOT ENOUGH

SCRIPTURE

"He gives strength to the weary and increases the power of the weak."

— Isaiah 40:29 (NIV)

Devotional

You try. You really do.

You wake up early — or at least earlier than you want to. You pour the cereal, sign the papers, change the diapers, reheat the coffee, and push through the day. You love your kids more than words can hold, but sometimes that love feels like it's not enough to keep up with the demands.

The tantrums drain you. The sibling fights wear you down. The appointments, the errands, the constant needs — they all pile on top of one another until you wonder if you're being crushed by your own life.

And underneath it all sits the question you don't want to say out loud:

What if I'm not enough for this?

It's the fear that keeps you up at night and follows you into the next day. It's the whisper behind the mom guilt, the mental overload, the occasional desire to run away to a quiet cabin in the woods. You give your best, but some days your best feels painfully inadequate .

Here's the truth: You're not enough. On your own, no human is. But that's not the end of the story — it's the beginning of grace.

God never asked you to be self-sufficient. He never expected you to carry this calling on your own strength. In fact, He knows you can't. That's why He promises to be the one who fills in the gaps, strengthens your hands, calms your heart, and carries what you can't.

You were never meant to be everything. You were meant to be *His* — dependent, rooted, and loved. Your weakness is not a problem to solve but a place where His power shines.

What if the moments when you feel inadequate are actually invitations? Invitations to draw near, to exhale, to let go of the impossible standard of "doing it all" and instead cling to the One who already did what you couldn't?

Your kids don't need a perfect mom. They need a present one. A real one. One who knows how to say, "I'm sorry," and, "Let's try again." One who admits her need for God and shows her children how to do the same.

So when that question comes — *What if I'm not enough?* — you can answer it with confidence:

"I'm not. But God is. And He is with me."

Prayer

Lord, I feel like I'm not enough. Some days, I feel like I'm failing in more ways than I can count. But You say that in my weakness, You are strong. Help me lean into Your strength. Remind me I don't have to do it all — I just have to come to You. Amen.

Weave It Into Your Day

Every time you feel overwhelmed this week, whisper, "He is enough." Let it become your quiet anthem of strength.

Week 5

GOD OF THE OVERFLOWING LAUNDRY BASKET

SCRIPTURE

"Cast all your anxiety on him because he cares for you."

— 1 Peter 5:7 (NIV)

Devotional

It never ends.

The laundry multiplies like it has a mind of its own. Just when you think you're caught up, someone tosses in a muddy pair of socks or spills orange juice down their shirt. The hampers are full, the dryer buzzer keeps going off, and you're pretty sure the only time the basket is ever empty is in your dreams.

And it's not just the laundry. It's the mental list — the appointments to make, the lunches to pack, the bills to pay, the groceries to grab, the school papers to sign. It all piles up. Some of it feels manageable, but a lot of it doesn't. Most days, you're carrying more than anyone realizes.

You know God is there, but it's hard to feel spiritual when you're sorting socks. It's hard to feel connected to Him when you're running in five directions and can't even remember if you ate lunch.

But what if God is already with you — not in spite of the mess, but right in the middle of it?

The laundry basket might seem like the least sacred object in your home, but maybe that's the exact place God wants to meet you. He doesn't ask you to come cleaned up and collected. He invites you to come as you are — buried in chores, worn out from giving, and still willing to turn your heart toward Him.

"Cast all your anxiety on him," Scripture says. Not just the big fears, but the everyday ones. The anxiety over time, the worry over money, the stress of holding it all together. God doesn't roll His eyes at your overwhelm. He cares. And He can carry the weight that's breaking your back.

There's no shame in being tired. There's no failure in needing rest. And there's nothing small about a mother who keeps showing up, load after load, day after day, in faithfulness and love.

So when you're sorting laundry this week — or sweeping up crumbs, or wiping down counters — remember this: you are not alone. Your effort is seen. Your heart is held. And the same God who split the sea and raised the dead is standing with you beside a basket of unfolded towels.

Prayer

Lord, I feel overwhelmed by the constant demands of life. Sometimes I forget that You care about the little things — even my messy laundry room. Help me to see Your presence in the middle of my routine and to lean on You when I feel like I'm drowning. Thank You for meeting me right here. Amen.

Weave It Into Your Day

As you do laundry this week, use that time to pray over each person in your household. Let each piece remind you: I serve in love, and God is with me.

Week 6

THE DEVOTION YOU DIDN'T PLAN

SCRIPTURE

"Very early in the morning, while it was still dark, Jesus got up, left the house and went off to a solitary place, where he prayed."

— Mark 1:35 (NIV)

Devotional

You had good intentions.

You set your alarm. You poured your coffee. You opened your Bible — maybe even lit a candle. But then someone woke up early. Someone needed breakfast, or had a nightmare, or couldn't find their other shoe. The moment you carved out for quiet with God was swallowed up by motherhood before it ever really began.

Maybe it's been weeks, even months, since you had a "real" quiet time — the kind with a journal, a highlighter, and some uninterrupted thought. And maybe you've started to feel a little distant, maybe even guilty. *Shouldn't I be doing more? Shouldn't I be more disciplined?*

But here's the grace: God is not limited to the moments you set aside. He shows up in the ones you didn't plan.

When Jesus slipped away to be alone with the Father, it wasn't because He found the perfect, uninterrupted window. It was often *before* sunrise, in the margins of already full days. Even then, people found Him. He was constantly interrupted — yet never disconnected from God.

You don't need a flawless routine to be close to Him. You don't need a peaceful house or a quiet room. God meets you where you are. He walks with you through the clutter, the noise, and the interruptions. He's not disappointed by your chaos — He steps into it with you.

That whisper of prayer while changing diapers? That moment of worship when you catch your child laughing? That breath of surrender when everything feels too loud? Those are real devotions. That's real connection.

Of course, intentional time with God is a beautiful goal. But He doesn't shame you for the season you're in. He knows the demands on your time. He knows the exhaustion that sits under your eyes. And He's not measuring your worth by your ability to highlight Scripture or fill a prayer journal.

He's measuring your heart — and your heart is still reaching for Him, even in the mess.

So the next time you feel like you've failed at being "spiritual," stop and remember: the devotion you didn't plan might be the one God uses the most.

Prayer

Father, I miss You — not because You've gone anywhere, but because I've been buried in the noise. Help me remember that You're still here. Even when I don't have a quiet space or a polished plan, meet me in the middle of the day. Let my scattered prayers and tired thoughts be enough for You. Amen.

Weave It Into Your Day

This week, talk to God in the middle of your routine — not before or after. Invite Him into what's already happening, and trust that He's listening.

Week 7

HE SEES YOU

SCRIPTURE

"'You are the God who sees me,' for she said, 'I have now seen the One who sees me.'"

— Genesis 16:13 (NIV)

Devotional

No one applauded when you cleaned the crumbs from under the table.

No one noticed when you folded the fourth load of laundry.

No one thanked you for remembering the field trip form, or for staying up late to fix the costume, or for showing up early — again.

Some days, motherhood can feel like a thankless loop. You pour out constantly, but the cup you're filling never seems full. You do what needs to be done, not for recognition, but because it's what love looks like. Still, there are moments when it stings — when it feels like no one sees how hard you're trying.

You don't need constant validation. But you do need to be reminded: you are not invisible. God sees you.

He sees the moments no one else notices — the midnight rocking, the whispered prayers, the weary sighs. He sees your patience when you want to snap. He sees your tears when the door is closed. He sees the way you put your child's needs before your own, again and again, even when you're running on fumes.

The story of Hagar in Genesis is a reminder that even in the wilderness — cast out, alone, and afraid — she was not forgotten. God met her there. He called her by name. And in awe, she gave Him the name El Roi: "The God who sees me."

You don't have to be in a literal desert to feel what Hagar felt. The middle years of motherhood can feel isolating. You're surrounded by little voices but often feel emotionally alone. You're constantly needed but rarely affirmed. It's easy to feel unseen — even by the people you love most.

But you are fully known. Fully loved. Fully seen.

God sees the sacrifices you make behind the scenes. The emotional weight you carry without complaint. The way you're growing, stretching, learning, and trying — even when it feels like no one notices. He is not distant. He is near. And He honors your faithfulness, even when it feels small.

You don't have to prove your worth or perform to be seen. You are already held in the eyes of a God who never looks away. So when you feel invisible, whisper this truth to your heart: *He sees me. And that is enough.*

Prayer

God, thank You for seeing me when I feel overlooked. Remind me that You are near, even when no one else notices. Help me find comfort in Your presence and strength in Your care. I want to live each day knowing that I matter to You — even in the smallest things. Amen.

Weave It Into Your Day

When no one notices what you do today, pause and say, "God sees this." Let His attention be enough for your heart.

Week 8

SANCTIFIED BY SIPPY CUPS AND SNACK BAGS

SCRIPTURE

"Being confident of this, that he who began a good work in you will carry it on to completion until the day of Christ Jesus."

— Philippians 1:6 (NIV)

Devotional

You used to dream about how motherhood would shape your children. What you didn't expect was how much it would shape *you*.

There's a kind of transformation that doesn't come from books or sermons or weekend retreats. It comes from early mornings, missed alarms, forgotten permission slips, after-school meltdowns, the hum of lunch prep, and the quiet, constant putting aside of your own plans to meet the needs of someone else.

It comes from pouring juice into a sippy cup while praying for patience — or packing another snack bag before sunrise.

It's in waiting for soccer practice to end when you'd rather be resting. In navigating friendship drama with your teen. In trying to be gentle when the attitude feels like too much. And in walking alongside them as they grow, while you're still growing too.

Motherhood is beautiful, yes — but it's also sanctifying. It presses on your weaknesses and tests your limits. It stretches your patience, reveals your pride, and confronts your desire for control. It shines a light on everything you'd rather hide — and brings your need for grace right to the surface.

And that's exactly where God meets you.

Sanctification is the lifelong process of becoming more like Jesus — not through perfection, but through surrender. It's not about striving harder or achieving a polished spiritual life. It's about letting God shape your heart in the middle of your real, messy, noisy, repetitive life.

You may not always recognize it, but growth is happening. Every time you choose gentleness instead of snapping, every time you show up with presence instead of guilt, every time you pray instead of panic — you are being transformed. Slowly. Quietly. Faithfully. Even on the days that feel like failures.

God does some of His best work in the trenches — in the repetition, the sacrifice, and the hidden spaces where no one sees but Him. You don't have to wait for life to calm down before He can use you. He's working through this exact season — in the carpool line, the spelling tests, the slammed doors, the soccer gear, the snack wrappers, and yes, even the leftover sippy cups still stacked in your cabinet.

You're not just raising kids. God is raising *you*, too.

Prayer

Father, thank You for meeting me in the middle of motherhood. Use even the messy, frustrating, and unglamorous moments to shape my heart. Grow me through each season, from sippy cups to teenage tears. Remind me that You are not finished with me yet. I trust You to keep working in me as I keep showing up. Amen.

Weave It Into Your Day

This week, when something interrupts your plan or stretches your patience, whisper: "God is growing me here." Let that truth shift your mindset and settle your soul.

PART TWO

Mom Identity: More Than a Title

❧

Motherhood has a way of reshaping everything—your time, your priorities, even your sense of self. Somewhere between diaper changes, carpool lines, and late-night worries, it's easy to lose sight of who *you* are.

But you are more than the tasks you complete and the titles you hold. You are not just a caretaker, a provider, or a problem-solver. You are **His**—fully known, fully loved, fully called.

This section is about remembering that your identity isn't swallowed up by motherhood. It's shaped by God's purpose for you. You are still growing, still becoming, still carrying dreams that matter. And through it all, God is carrying *you*.

You are not "just" a mom. You are His. And that changes everything.

Week 9

WHO AM I (BESIDES MOM)?

SCRIPTURE

"For you are God's masterpiece, created in Christ Jesus to do good works, which God prepared in advance for us to do."

— Ephesians 2:10 (NIV)

Devotional

You hear your name all day long — *Mom, Mommy, Mama*. Sometimes it's sweet. Sometimes it's shouted. Sometimes it's repeated so many times you forget you even had another name.

And that's part of the beauty of motherhood — to be so deeply known and needed. But somewhere in the blur of permission slips, carpool lines, and dinner prep, you might quietly start to wonder:

Who am I, besides Mom?

It's not that you resent the title. It's sacred. You carry it with love. But the person underneath still matters. The woman with passions and gifts and longings. The one who used to write or dance or laugh loudly at her own jokes. The one who once had a name badge or passport or playlist that had nothing to do with kids.

Motherhood doesn't erase who you were. It just adds new layers. But those original pieces? They're still part of you. You are not only a mom. You are a daughter of God — His masterpiece. Created in Christ Jesus. Designed for a life full of purpose, not just in what you do for others, but in who you are becoming.

God sees all of you — not just the mom parts. He sees the late-night thinker, the creative soul, the leader, the listener, the dreamer. And He doesn't expect you to leave those pieces behind. He invites you to bring them with you into this season, even if they look different than they once did.

Maybe the dreams look smaller right now, or slower. Maybe your gifts are used in different ways — in how you comfort a child, plan a family night, or encourage another mom who's barely hanging on. But those things still matter. You still matter.

There will come a time — sooner than it feels — when your children won't need you in quite the same way. When the house will be quieter and the calendar more open. And when that time comes, you'll want to remember the woman you were before the constant noise. Not to go backward, but to move forward — whole, rooted, and still growing.

So yes, you're Mom. But that's not your only name. You are a beloved creation, handcrafted by God with purpose and intention. Don't lose sight of the woman underneath the title. She's still here. And she still matters.

Prayer

Lord, thank You for the gift of motherhood — and for seeing me as more than the roles I carry. Remind me that I am Your creation, with a name and purpose that go beyond the daily tasks. Help me rediscover the woman You made me to be. Amen.

Weave It Into Your Day

Write down five words that describe you that don't involve your role as a mom. Ask God to help you nurture those parts of yourself again.

Week 10

YOUR NAME IS STILL YOURS

SCRIPTURE

"'Fear not, for I have redeemed you; I have summoned you by name; you are mine."

— Isaiah 43:1b (NIV)

Devotional

There was a time when your name stood on its own.

Not as someone's mom. Not as "So-and-so's wife." Just you — your first and last name, unmodified and unlinked to anyone else. Maybe you signed it at work, wore it on a name tag, or scribbled it on the corner of a notebook just because it felt good to see it in ink.

Now it's mostly "Mom," and it's beautiful. It's one of the most sacred titles a person can carry. But some days, if you're honest, it's easy to feel like you've disappeared beneath it.

Like your identity has become a collection of job descriptions: chef, chauffeur, nurse, referee, tutor, counselor, manager, cleaner, comforter — and the list goes on. You've taken on all of these roles with love, but sometimes, you forget that there's a person underneath them all. A name. A soul.

And God has never forgotten.

He still calls you by *your* name — not just your title. When He speaks to your heart, He doesn't say, "Hey, Mom." He calls you by the name He gave you before the world redefined you with responsibilities. He sees you fully, not just as who you are to others, but as who you are to Him.

"You are mine," He says in Isaiah. Not "You belong to your kids," or "You exist to hold everyone else together," but simply, "You are mine." He summoned you by name, long before the car seats and play dates and chaos.

And here's the quiet truth: your name still matters. Your voice, your passions, your calling — they're not lost. Maybe they've been buried or quieted. Maybe you've poured so much out that you've forgotten what fills *you* back up.

But God hasn't forgotten. And He's still working in you, not just through what you do, but through who you are.

You don't have to wait until the kids are grown to reclaim the woman inside the mom. She's still here. She's being refined, deepened, stretched. And God is still calling her forward — by name.

So today, take a moment to remember: your name is still yours. And the God who knows it also knows everything you carry. He sees the layers, the love, the fatigue, and the effort. He sees *you*.

Prayer

Lord, thank You for knowing me by name — even when I forget who I am outside of what I do. Help me reconnect with the woman You created me to be. Remind me that I am Yours, not just in title or task, but in identity. Help me live from that truth today. Amen.

Weave It Into Your Day

Say your full name aloud every day this week. Let it remind you that you are still your own person — deeply known, deeply loved, and not forgotten.

Week 11

CALLED, NOT JUST TIRED

SCRIPTURE

"Let us not become weary in doing good, for at the proper time we will reap a harvest if we do not give up."

— Galatians 6:9 (NIV)

Devotional

You're tired. Not just physically, though that's part of it. You're tired in your bones. In your thoughts. In your spirit.

You're tired of the endless meals and messes. Tired of repeating yourself. Tired of carrying so many people's needs, moods, and expectations while trying not to lose your grip on your own. Some days you wonder how you're supposed to keep going when you're already stretched thin.

And in the middle of all this exhaustion, you may start to believe a quiet lie: *This is all I am now. Just tired. Just surviving. Just going through the motions.*

But friend, you're not *just tired*. You are *called*.

You have been handpicked by God to mother these exact children in this exact season. That's not random. That's divine. And while it doesn't erase the fatigue or make the hard days easy, it changes the way you see them. It reminds you that even the smallest, most exhausting acts of service carry eternal significance.

When Paul wrote to the Galatians, he didn't say, "Try not to be tired." He said, "Don't grow weary in doing good." That implies the tiredness is real — but so is the purpose. So is the promise of a harvest.

There is good in what you're doing. There is beauty in the mundane — like packing lunches when you'd rather go back to bed, like holding space for your teenager's silence, like folding laundry at midnight... God sees your steady hands and selfless choices. He sees the tired woman behind the to-do list, and He whispers to her heart: *You are doing holy work.*

You're not doing these things because you have endless energy. You're doing them because love compels you. And where love leads, God strengthens.

Being called doesn't mean being constantly inspired. It means showing up, even when it's hard. It means trusting that your offering — however small or sleepy — matters. And it means remembering that you're not running this race alone. God is walking beside you, renewing your strength with every step.

So no, you're not just tired. You're *tired and called*. And that calling? It's sustained not by your strength, but by His.

Prayer

Lord, I'm weary. Some days I feel like I have nothing left to give. Remind me that You've called me to this season — not to do it perfectly, but to walk with You through it. Strengthen me in the weariness, and help me trust that You're growing something good. Amen.

Weave It Into Your Day

This week, as you go through your routine, repeat this truth: "I'm not just tired. I'm called." Let that reminder carry you.

Week 12

BECOMING WHILE RAISING

SCRIPTURE

"For we are God's handiwork, created in Christ Jesus to do good works, which God prepared in advance for us to do."

— Ephesians 2:10 (NIV)

Devotional

You spend a lot of time thinking about who your children are becoming. You watch for signs of growth — in how they handle frustration, show kindness, or take responsibility. You want to raise them well, help them flourish, and launch them into the world with strong character and a sense of purpose.

But how often do you pause and consider that *you're still becoming,* too?

It's easy to forget that God is shaping *you* in the middle of raising them. You're not a finished product. You're not just holding space for someone else's development — you're actively growing, changing, and being transformed through every stage of motherhood.

Every hard conversation that stretches your patience, every sleepless night that tests your endurance, every act of selflessness that requires surrender — these are all tools God is using to refine you. You are becoming wiser, gentler, more grounded in grace. It might not feel like growth, especially on the hard days, but God is working under the surface.

You are God's handiwork, too.

Your identity isn't frozen in the version of yourself that existed before kids. And it isn't limited to "Mom," either. You are a woman being shaped by the hand of a loving Creator. You are allowed to keep dreaming, learning, evolving — even in the middle of minivans and messes.

Sometimes motherhood feels like pressing pause on your own life, but God doesn't hit pause on your growth just because you're focused on others. He multiplies it. He uses the highs and lows of family life to draw out the kind of fruit that lasts — patience, compassion, humility, wisdom, and joy.

And the beauty of this is that your kids get to see it happening in real time. They don't just watch you take care of them — they see you becoming more like Christ. They witness what it looks like to keep growing, to stay humble, to admit when you're wrong, to keep going when you're weary. What a powerful example that sets.

You're not done yet. The version of you five years from now will look different from who you are today — not because you've finally arrived, but because you kept becoming. And God? He'll still be right there, guiding the journey, growing you both.

Prayer

Father, thank You that I'm still becoming. Even in this busy season of raising others, You haven't stopped shaping me. Help me to embrace the process and trust that You're doing something beautiful — even when I can't see it yet. Grow me as I guide others, and let me become more like You. Amen.

Weave It Into Your Day

Take a moment to reflect: How have I grown in the past year? Give God thanks for shaping you, even in the midst of the chaos.

Week 13

WHEN YOUR DREAMS ARE ON HOLD

SCRIPTURE

"Trust in the Lord with all your heart and lean not on your own understanding; in all your ways submit to him, and he will make your paths straight."

— Proverbs 3:5–6 (NIV)

Devotional

You didn't stop dreaming. You just put some of them on hold.

Maybe it was the career path you planned to pursue. The book you wanted to write. The business idea you were just starting to shape. Or maybe it wasn't about a project at all — maybe it was the dream of rest, of space, of something that felt like *yours*.

And then motherhood happened — and with it came a thousand beautiful, exhausting detours. Your hands filled with tiny socks and lunchboxes. Your calendar filled with practices and appointments. Your mind filled with worries about everyone else.

You love your children deeply. You wouldn't trade this season for anything. But sometimes, a quiet ache surfaces — a wondering about what happened to the parts of yourself that had plans, hopes, longings of their own. The guilt creeps in just for thinking it. But it's there, and it's real.

Let this be your permission to feel both: joy and longing. Gratitude and grief. Contentment and desire.

God is not surprised by your dreams. He's the One who wired you to care, to create, to build and grow things — not just children, but ideas and passions, too. And He's not angry that those dreams are still alive inside you. He planted many of them Himself.

But here's the key: sometimes God asks us to wait. Not because the dream is wrong — but because He's shaping us first. There are seasons for planting, and seasons for growing, and seasons for pausing while the roots go deep beneath the surface.

Your pause is not your punishment. Your delay is not your denial.

There may be dreams that unfold later — after the baby years, after high school graduations, after this current chapter closes. But there may also be ways God wants to breathe life into your longings *now*, in small and unexpected forms. Don't be afraid to ask Him.

Trust doesn't mean giving up. It means loosening your grip and letting God hold the timeline. It means believing that the Creator who knit your motherhood journey together also cares about your personal hopes — even the ones that feel buried right now.

You're not forgotten. Neither are your dreams. Keep showing up. Keep trusting. And when the time is right, He will make a way.

Prayer

God, You see the dreams in my heart — the ones I've delayed, dismissed, or buried. Help me trust Your timing. Remind me that You're not finished writing my story, and that no part of who I am is wasted. Give me peace in the waiting and courage to hope again. Amen.

Weave It Into Your Day

Take five minutes to write down a dream that still lives in your heart. Offer it to God, and ask Him to hold it with you.

Week 14

SHE LAUGHS AT THE DAYS TO COME

SCRIPTURE

"She is clothed with strength and dignity; she can laugh at the days to come."

— Proverbs 31:25 (NIV)

Devotional

There's a lot about the future that can feel overwhelming.

Will my kids be okay? Will they stay close to God? Will they find their way? Will I?

You think about the next phase — high school, college, adulthood — and sometimes it stirs up more fear than excitement. The what-ifs creep in. The stakes feel high. And in a world that moves fast and changes constantly, it's easy to carry quiet anxiety about what's around the corner.

But then there's this line from Proverbs 31. A woman of wisdom, strength, and dignity "laughs at the days to come." Not because life is easy or predictable, but because she knows something deeper: *God is already there.*

This kind of laughter isn't careless or naïve. It's not the laughter of denial or pretending everything will go perfectly. It's the quiet, confident laughter of someone who trusts the One who holds the future. It's the kind that says, *I don't know what's coming, but I know Who walks with me through it.*

The truth is, much of motherhood is lived in the in-between — between what is and what's still to come. You're planting seeds now that won't bloom for years. You're teaching lessons, praying hard, and hoping something sticks. You don't get immediate results. You don't always get reassurance. But you do get God — steady, faithful, unchanging.

And when the future feels uncertain, that's where your strength lies. Not in your ability to control the outcome, but in your ability to trust the God who's never failed you yet.

You can laugh at the days to come not because you know what they'll hold, but because you know Who will be holding *you.* That's not shallow optimism. That's deep, durable faith.

So when the worries rise — when the news headlines scare you, when your child makes a mistake, when the unknown looms large — you don't have to spiral. You can pause, breathe, and smile at what's ahead, knowing that none of it will surprise God. He's already making a way. He's already working behind the scenes. And He'll be there, just like He is today.

Prayer

God, the future feels so big sometimes. Help me release the parts I can't control and trust that You are already there. Teach me to face tomorrow with peace, not fear. Let my faith grow stronger than my worry. Thank You for walking with me every step of the way — yesterday, today, and forever. Amen.

Weave It Into Your Day

Look ahead to something on your calendar that makes you feel anxious. Pause and whisper, "God is already there." Let that truth soften your fear and steady your heart.

Week 15

YOU'RE NOT DOING IT WRONG

SCRIPTURE

"Therefore encourage one another and build each other up, just as in fact you are doing."

— 1 Thessalonians 5:11 (NIV)

Devotional

There are days when it feels like everyone else has it figured out.

One mom posts chore charts that actually work. Another seems to cook from scratch every night. There's the one who's always on time, the one with the organized schedule, and the one whose kids are already learning a second language while you're just trying to find clean socks.

Comparison sneaks in quietly. It doesn't shout. It whispers: *You're behind. You're not doing enough. You're doing it wrong.*

And once that thought takes root, it's hard to shake. You start second-guessing everything — your discipline, your routines, your pace, your parenting style. You wonder if your house should be quieter or your life more structured. You question if you're giving your kids what they need or somehow falling short.

But here's the truth: you're not doing it wrong. You're doing it *your* way — the way that fits your family, your rhythm, your values, and your season. And that's not just okay — it's *right*.

There is no one-size-fits-all formula for motherhood. Your home doesn't have to look like anyone else's. Your pace doesn't have to match your friend's. Your parenting style doesn't have to check every box from every book. What matters most is love — and you've got that in spades.

God didn't give your children to a perfect parent. He gave them to *you*. On purpose. With your personality, your quirks, your strengths, your imperfections. He knew exactly what He was doing. And He's not grading you on performance — He's walking with you through the process.

When Paul told the Thessalonians to encourage and build one another up, he added an important note: "just as in fact you are doing." Sometimes we need that same reminder. You're not failing. You're already doing more right than you realize.

Yes, there's always room to grow — but that doesn't mean you're doing it wrong now. It just means God is still working, shaping, and refining you along the way.

So the next time you see a picture-perfect post or hear another mom's success story and feel that familiar twist of doubt, pause. Remind yourself: *God didn't ask me to be her. He asked me to be me.*

Prayer

Lord, help me silence the voices of comparison and listen to Your voice instead. Remind me that I'm not failing just because my life doesn't look like someone else's. Thank You for equipping me to love my family in the way only I can. Help me rest in the truth that I'm not doing it wrong — I'm doing it with You. Amen.

Weave It Into Your Day

Write down three things you're doing well in motherhood right now. Keep the list somewhere visible this week as a quiet reminder: you're doing better than you think.

Week 16

CARRIED AND CALLED

SCRIPTURE

"I have made you and I will carry you; I will sustain you and I will rescue you."

— Isaiah 46:4b (NIV)

Devotional

There's something about motherhood that makes you feel like you need to carry it all.

You carry schedules, emotions, school projects, groceries, laundry, and expectations — not to mention the mental checklist that never quite turns off. You carry worry and responsibility. You carry other people's needs in front of your own. And some days, you carry the quiet fear that you're not doing enough.

The weight gets heavy. And while you don't say it out loud, there are moments when you wonder how long you can keep this up without falling apart.

But here's the good news: you were never meant to carry it all alone.

Before you were a mother, you were a daughter. And God, your loving Father, never stopped seeing you that way. He didn't just call you to this season — He promised to *carry* you through it.

In Isaiah, God reminds His people that He's not only the one who made them — He's the one who will sustain them. He doesn't walk behind you with a clipboard, waiting for you to get it right. He walks beside you, shoulder to shoulder, heart to heart. When your strength fails, His does not.

Yes, you've been called to something important — something sacred. But God didn't assign you this mission and then step away. He is involved in every detail, from the sleepless nights to the hard conversations. He sees the invisible work and honors it. He sees your tears and holds them. He knows when you're barely holding it together — and He holds *you*.

Being called doesn't mean being capable on your own. It means being dependent — and that's where freedom begins. You don't have to be everything. You don't have to carry the whole world. You just have to walk with the One who already has.

So breathe. You are carried, even as you carry others. And you are called, not because you're strong enough, but because God's strength is made perfect in your weakness. He chose *you* for this — and He's not letting go.

Prayer

Father, I'm carrying so much. Sometimes it feels like more than I can handle. Thank You for reminding me that I don't have to do it all in my own strength. You made me, You called me, and You promised to carry me. Help me trust You more deeply and lean on You more freely. Thank You for being faithful every step of the way. Amen.

Weave It Into Your Day

Close your eyes and visualize handing over what feels heaviest right now — a worry, a burden, a fear. Imagine God receiving it, and feel the relief of not having to carry it alone.

PART THREE

Patience, Peace, and Prayer

Some days, you wake up already running on empty. The demands are endless, the noise is nonstop, and your patience feels thinner than your last night's sleep. You try to pray, but your thoughts are scattered. You long for peace, but life keeps pulling at you from every direction.

This section is for those days—the ones that require more grace than you have, more patience than you can muster, and more peace than your circumstances allow.

Here's the good news: you don't have to generate these things on your own. God meets you in the mess, supplying what you lack. Your hurried, distracted prayers still reach Him. Your deep sighs count as surrender. And even in the middle of the chaos, His peace is available —not because everything is perfect, but because *He* is present.

When patience runs out, when prayer feels weak, when peace seems impossible—He is still enough. And He is with you, every step of the way.

Week 17

PRAYING WHILE STIRRING PASTA

Scripture

"Pray continually."

— 1 Thessalonians 5:17 (NIV)

Devotional

Sometimes prayer looks like a quiet morning and an open Bible. But other times? It looks like talking to God while stirring pasta, wiping counters, and answering a hundred questions in a row.

There's this idea floating around that prayer has to be polished — set apart in time and space, uninterrupted and reverent. And while those quiet, intentional moments are beautiful and important, they're not the only way to connect with God.

Sometimes the only time you get to pray is when dinner is boiling over and your kid is melting down and you whisper, "Lord, help me," with one hand on the spoon and the other holding everything else together.

And the good news? That counts.

God is not only present in your structured devotion time. He's just as near in the noisy kitchen, in the cluttered living room, in the carpool line, in the grocery store aisle. He's not waiting for you to have more time — He's ready to meet you in the time you have.

"Pray continually," Paul writes in 1 Thessalonians. Not because prayer is one more task to complete, but because it's the rhythm that sustains your soul. It's the constant undercurrent, the quiet conversation that keeps you grounded, even when the rest of life feels like chaos.

You don't need perfect words. You don't need long stretches of silence. You just need a heart that turns toward Him again and again — in the small moments, in the frustrations, in the gratitude, and even in the boredom.

God isn't grading your eloquence. He's listening to your heart.

So talk to Him while you cook. Pray over the meal, yes — but also pray over the hands that will eat it. Pray for peace to fill your home. Pray for patience to meet your stress. Pray for your children's friendships, fears, futures. Pray that they will come to know the One you're whispering to in the middle of the mess.

Your kitchen can be sacred ground. Your dinner prep can be a holy moment. Not because it's calm or quiet, but because *you're turning your heart toward God in the middle of it.*

That's what makes prayer powerful — not the setting, but the connection.

Prayer

Lord, thank You for meeting me in the middle of my day, not just in the quiet corners. Help me to talk to You freely — while I work, while I cook, while I go about the ordinary. Teach me to make prayer a part of everything, even when nothing feels particularly spiritual. Thank You for being close. Amen.

Weave It Into Your Day

While preparing a meal this week, pause and offer a short prayer — for your family, for peace, or simply to say thank You. Let that moment reset your heart.

Week 18

THE PATIENCE YOU DON'T HAVE

SCRIPTURE

"But the fruit of the Spirit is love, joy, peace, patience, kindness, goodness, faithfulness, gentleness and self-control."

— Galatians 5:22–23a (NIV)

Devotional

It always seems to happen when you're running late.

One child can't find their shoes. Another refuses to wear pants. There's a mysterious spill by the door, the dog starts barking, and someone asks you a deep question about the afterlife right as you're trying to zip a backpack.

You snap. Or sigh. Or mutter something you instantly regret. And there it is again — the familiar frustration that you just don't have enough patience for this. You're not alone.

Patience may be a virtue, but it doesn't always come naturally — especially in motherhood. In fact, some days it feels like patience is the one thing you need most and have the least. You want to stay calm. You want to respond with grace. But your bandwidth is stretched, your nerves are fried, and your coffee got cold an hour ago.

The beautiful (and humbling) truth is that patience isn't something you have to generate on your own. According to Galatians, it's not a personality trait or a skill you master — it's a *fruit of the Spirit*. That means it's something God grows in you, not something you grind out by willpower.

And like all fruit, it takes time to ripen.

You won't wake up one day with limitless calm. But as you walk with God — in the mess, in the noise, in the thousand small decisions of your day — His Spirit produces something in you that wasn't there before. Not perfectly. Not instantly. But *faithfully*.

Your outbursts don't disqualify you from growth. They simply remind you that you still need Jesus — and that's exactly where transformation begins.

So instead of shaming yourself for the moments you lose it, bring those moments to God. Invite Him in. Ask Him to help you pause before reacting. Ask Him to slow your breathing and soften your tone. Ask Him to grow patience in you, even if it comes in slow, steady increments.

And when you do respond with more peace than you expected — when you bite your tongue, take a breath, or offer grace instead of anger — pause and give thanks. That's not just maturity. That's evidence that the Spirit is at work in you.

You may not feel patient. But you are being made new.

Prayer

Lord, I confess I don't have the patience I wish I had. I get overwhelmed and frustrated so easily. Please grow this fruit in me — not by my strength, but by Your Spirit. Help me to pause, breathe, and respond with grace, even when everything feels chaotic. Thank You for not giving up on me. Amen.

Weave It Into Your Day

Pick one moment today to intentionally pause before reacting. Even a deep breath can be a spiritual act of surrender.

Week 19

HOLY INTERRUPTIONS

SCRIPTURE

"In their hearts humans plan their course, but the Lord establishes their steps."

— Proverbs 16:9 (NIV)

Devotional

You had a plan for today. Maybe even a good one — productive, balanced, with a little breathing room built in. But before you could even check off the first item, life showed up loud and unexpected.

A child needed something. A spill slowed you down. An email derailed your schedule. A tantrum or a phone call or a last-minute school reminder turned your neat little plan into a crumpled list of undone intentions. And that's just the first hour.

Motherhood is full of interruptions. Some small. Some jarring. And when you're already running low on energy or margin, those interruptions don't feel holy — they feel like the last straw.

But what if interruptions are sometimes the very places where God wants to meet us?

Jesus was interrupted constantly. People stopped Him in crowds. Friends interrupted His rest. Strangers reached out in desperation. Children ran to Him when others tried to send them away. And not once did He brush them off. Instead, He often used those interruptions to reveal something important — to show compassion, heal brokenness, or speak truth into a moment.

He didn't live on a rigid schedule. He lived with open hands. And that allowed Him to see that sometimes the interruption *was* the assignment.

Your time and energy matter. It's okay to feel frustrated when your plans fall apart. But don't miss the moments that might actually be invitations. That question in the hallway, that unexpected hug, that meltdown at bedtime — they might be holy ground, if you let them be.

Interruptions don't always feel spiritual. But they often bring us face to face with our limits — and in that space, we discover again how much we need God. They slow us down, humble us, and sometimes even soften us. They peel back our plans so God's presence can break through.

Yes, you can still make a plan. God doesn't ask us to live in chaos. But when the plan unravels, remember: He's still in control. He's not surprised. And He's still working — in you and through you — even when the day looks nothing like you expected.

Prayer

Lord, I get frustrated when my plans are interrupted. Help me to hold my schedule loosely and trust that You are at work in the interruptions. Teach me to slow down, to see people the way You do, and to meet each unexpected moment with grace. Amen.

Weave It Into Your Day

This week, when something interrupts your plans, pause and ask: "What does God want to show me here?" Let curiosity replace frustration — even just for a moment.

Week 20

BREATHE IN, BREATHE OUT, BELIEVE

SCRIPTURE

"The Lord gives strength to his people; the Lord blesses his people with peace."

— Psalm 29:11 (NIV)

Devotional

Sometimes all you can do is breathe.

You can't solve the meltdown. You can't clean the whole house. You can't figure out how to juggle everything waiting on your plate. You don't even have the words to pray. All you have is breath — one inhale, one exhale at a time.

And that's more than enough.

Breath is sacred. It's what God used to bring life into the first human. It's what sustains you when everything feels like too much. And it's one of the simplest ways to come back to His presence — not through performance, but through stillness.

Inhale: *God is here.* Exhale: *I am not alone.* Inhale: *He gives me strength.* Exhale: *He gives me peace.*

You don't need to escape to a mountaintop to experience God. Sometimes all it takes is slowing down enough to feel your breath and remember the truth: you are not holding your life together — He is.

So much of motherhood happens in motion. You're moving from task to task, need to need, day to day. But your soul wasn't made to run nonstop. God wired you for rhythm — work and rest, pouring out and being filled.

When you ignore that rhythm for too long, your spirit starts to fray. You get snappy, numb, anxious, or just deeply, deeply tired. And what you need most isn't more willpower or a better system — it's a pause. A deep breath. A moment of reconnection with the One who sees you and still holds you close.

The good news? That moment is never far away.

You can breathe Him in while waiting at a red light, folding a towel, or hiding in the bathroom for thirty seconds of quiet. You can reconnect not by doing more, but by doing less — just enough to say, *God, I need You. Please steady me again.*

It won't fix everything. But it might shift something inside you — just enough to keep going. Just enough to move forward in peace instead of panic. Because peace isn't the absence of stress. It's the presence of God, even in the middle of it.

So today, when you feel overwhelmed, don't push harder. Don't try to "power through." Just stop for a moment. Breathe in. Breathe out. Believe.

Prayer

Lord, when I feel overwhelmed, help me pause and breathe. Remind me that You are near, that You are strong, and that You are with me. I don't need to have it all together — I just need to remember that I'm not alone. Fill me with Your peace today. Amen.

Weave It Into Your Day

Set a timer for one minute. Inhale slowly. Exhale even slower. With each breath, whisper a simple prayer: "God, give me peace."

Week 21

WHAT TO DO WITH MOM GUILT

SCRIPTURE

"There is now no condemnation for those who are in Christ Jesus."

— Romans 8:1 (NIV)

Devotional

It shows up at the end of a long day — or in the middle of one that just started. That sinking feeling that you didn't do enough, say it right, or handle things the way you "should have."

Maybe you lost your patience. Maybe you missed something important. Maybe your child seemed sad or distant, and you're not even sure why. Or maybe nothing happened — and *still* the guilt lingers.

Mom guilt is sneaky like that. It attaches itself to things big and small. And if left unchecked, it will convince you that you are always falling short, no matter how hard you try.

But here's the truth: guilt is meant to be a signal, not a sentence. It's something to bring to God — not something to carry like a badge of shame.

Sometimes guilt shows us where we need to make things right — to apologize, to grow, to ask for help. That's healthy. But other times, guilt is just the voice of fear or perfectionism in disguise. It tells you that unless you do everything flawlessly, you've failed. That voice is *not* from God.

Romans reminds us that in Christ, there is no condemnation. None. Zero. That includes condemnation over your parenting. If you are in Him, you are covered — fully, freely, forever.

You're going to make mistakes. That's not a surprise to God. He didn't choose you to be a mom because He thought you'd never mess up. He chose you knowing your weakness — and also knowing that His grace would be more than enough. So what do you do with the guilt?

You bring it into the light. You ask, *Is this conviction from God? Or pressure I've put on myself?* If it's conviction, lean in. Repent. Make things right. If it's shame or fear or comparison — let it go.

Remind yourself when the guilt creeps in: I am loved. I am forgiven. I am learning. I am not alone. I am not perfect— and I don't have to be.

The best gift you can give your kids isn't perfection. It's a mom who models humility, honesty, and grace — toward them and toward herself. And that starts with how you handle the weight of guilt.

You don't have to carry it anymore.

Prayer

God, You know where I feel like I've fallen short. Thank You for loving me anyway. Show me the difference between healthy conviction and toxic shame. Help me receive Your grace and give that same grace to myself. I want to walk in freedom, not fear. Thank You for never condemning me. Amen.

Weave It Into Your Day

Think of one thing you're feeling guilty about today. Say it out loud, then say: "I give this to You, God. I will not carry what You've already forgiven."

Week 22

⌒✲⌒

WHEN PRAYER FEELS POINTLESS

SCRIPTURE

"Then Jesus told his disciples a parable to show them that they should always pray and not give up."

— Luke 18:1 (NIV)

Devotional

You've prayed for sleep — and still been awake all night.

You've prayed for peace — and still faced conflict before breakfast.

You've prayed for wisdom, strength, breakthrough, patience — and some days, it just feels like nothing changes.

Maybe you've whispered prayers in the middle of chaos, but it didn't make the chaos stop. Maybe you've begged God for help, only to feel like you're still holding everything together with shaky hands. And maybe you've started to wonder: *What's the point?*

If you've ever felt like prayer is more effort than outcome, you're not alone. Even the most faithful believers hit seasons when prayer feels hard, hollow, or unproductive.

But here's the quiet truth: prayer was never meant to be a formula that guarantees instant results. It's a relationship. A lifeline. A posture of your heart toward the One who already knows and still listens.

In Luke 18, Jesus tells a parable to encourage His disciples to always pray and not give up. Not because the answers would always come quickly. But because *persistence in prayer builds intimacy, trust, and transformation* — even when circumstances don't change right away.

Sometimes prayer doesn't fix the moment — it anchors you in it. It steadies your hands when they're trembling. It reminds you that you're not carrying this alone. It opens the door for peace to walk in, even if the problem stays right where it is.

And sometimes? The act of praying is the miracle itself. Because in that moment, your heart is choosing connection over despair. Surrender over control. Faith over frustration.

You don't need perfect words. You don't need eloquence or structure. You just need willingness — the courage to keep showing up, even when it feels like nothing is happening. Because something *is* happening, even if you can't see it yet.

God hears. God sees. God responds — sometimes in ways you'll only understand later. But He's never ignoring you.

So when prayer feels pointless, pray anyway. Not because you have to, but because you *get to*. Because He's still listening. And He's still near.

Prayer

God, sometimes prayer feels hard. I wonder if You're listening, if You care, or if anything will ever change. But I choose to keep coming back. Remind me that You are close, even when I don't feel it. Grow my faith in the waiting. Anchor me in Your presence, and teach me to trust again. Amen.

Weave It Into Your Day

Set a timer for three minutes. Don't try to "pray right." Just talk to God about whatever's on your heart. Keep it honest, messy, real — and trust that He's listening.

Week 23

PEACE IN PIECES

Scripture

"Peace I leave with you; my peace I give you. I do not give to you as the world gives. Do not let your hearts be troubled and do not be afraid."

— John 14:27 (NIV)

Devotional

You keep looking for that elusive moment — the one where everything is calm, the house is clean, the to-do list is finished, and no one needs anything. You imagine yourself finally able to exhale, to feel peace settle over you like a blanket.

But that moment? It rarely shows up. If it does, it lasts five minutes — maybe less — before something spills, someone cries, or another need comes calling.

It's easy to believe peace only lives in the quiet. That it requires silence, stillness, or everything being in order. But Jesus offers a different kind of peace — one that's not dependent on your circumstances, but anchored in His presence.

"Peace I leave with you," He said. "My peace I give you. I do not give to you as the world gives."

The world gives temporary peace — the kind that comes when everything is just right. But Jesus gives *permanent peace* — the kind that can live inside of you even when everything around you is messy, loud, and unresolved.

Peace in pieces.

It's not all-or-nothing. Sometimes it's found in slivers — in a deep breath before you respond. In a whispered prayer while folding laundry. In a moment of eye contact with your child that reminds you both you're still connected.

Peace is found in the presence of God, not the absence of problems.

That means you don't have to wait until life is perfect to feel it. You don't have to wait until bedtime, vacation, or a "better season." You can experience it now — one moment at a time, one prayer at a time, one piece at a time.

Some days peace will be obvious. Other days you'll have to look for it. But the promise remains: Jesus offers you a peace the world cannot manufacture or take away. And He gives it *in pieces*, not to tease you, but to remind you that He is here — even in the smallest corners of your day.

So stop chasing a perfect scenario and start welcoming the presence of a perfect Savior. He's in your kitchen. In your car. In your chaos. And His peace is real — even in the pieces.

Prayer

Jesus, I keep waiting for things to calm down so I can feel peace. But You offer something better — peace that lives in me, no matter what's going on around me. Help me stop chasing perfection and start receiving Your presence in the middle of my messy days. Let Your peace meet me in pieces, and let those pieces be enough. Amen.

Weave It Into Your Day

Look for one "piece of peace" each day — a small moment of calm, connection, or joy. Pause to thank God for it. Let it be a reminder that He is near.

Week 24

THE LONG VIEW

Scripture

"For I will pour water on the thirsty land, and streams on the dry ground; I will pour out my Spirit on your offspring, and my blessing on your descendants."

— Isaiah 44:3 (NIV)

Devotional

Motherhood has a way of narrowing your focus. You get caught in the dailiness of it all — packing lunches, wiping counters, signing forms, solving conflicts. You move from one urgent need to the next, barely catching your breath. And somewhere along the way, your faith can start to feel just as dry and stretched as your schedule.

You still believe. You still love God. But maybe it's been a while since you felt truly connected to Him. You pray in quick bursts, you skim devotionals instead of soaking in Scripture, and your heart often feels... flat. Not angry. Not rebellious. Just tired.

This is where *the long view* matters.

Faith is not measured in moments. It's measured in movement — slow, steady, imperfect movement toward the heart of God. Some seasons are rich and vibrant. Others feel like desert places. But God is in both.

In Isaiah, God promises to pour out water on dry ground — not just to satisfy, but to *restore*. He doesn't shame the thirsty. He meets them. He sends streams to cracked, barren places and breathes life where there was none. And He does it over time, with grace and patience.

God sees the long view. He's not anxious about your season. He knows where He's leading you, and He's not in a rush. He is far more committed to your transformation than to your temporary performance.

The truth is, faith deepens when it's lived over years — through discipline, repetition, and trust that holds even when the feelings fade. Your soul may not always feel on fire, but your roots can still grow deep. And often, the most lasting growth happens quietly beneath the surface.

The same is true for your children. You won't see fruit from every lesson or prayer or boundary you set. Not right away. But the seeds are there. And with time, they'll bloom.

So lift your eyes from the chaos of this week and look further down the road. God isn't finished with you. He's not finished with them. And the season you're in now is not the whole story.

Take the long view. And trust the One who holds every part of the journey.

Prayer

God, I feel dry sometimes. I want to feel close to You, but the noise and weight of life make it hard. Thank You for seeing the bigger picture. Help me to trust that You are working — even in the dry seasons — and to walk with You, one faithful step at a time. Amen.

Weave It Into Your Day

Today, pause and imagine your faith five years from now — stronger, deeper, quieter, but rooted. Thank God for how He's growing you, even now.

PART FOUR
Love in the Trenches

Loving your child is easy. But loving them *well*—with patience, wisdom, and grace—when you're exhausted, overwhelmed, or frustrated? That's the real challenge.

This section is for the moments when love feels costly. When you're managing meltdowns, backtalk, discipline, and your own emotions all at once. When you're grieving how fast they're growing or wrestling with anger you didn't know you had. When you're caught between wanting control and needing to trust God instead.

Motherhood is deep love, deep exhaustion, and deep grace all tangled together. The hard moments don't mean you're failing—they mean you're in the trenches, doing the sacred work of showing up, again and again. And through it all, God is with you, ready to supply the love, patience, and mercy you need.

Because even in the hardest moments, love is still worth choosing. And you don't have to choose it alone.

Week 25

STAYING STILL IN THE STORM

SCRIPTURE

"The Lord is close to the brokenhearted and saves those who are crushed in spirit."

— Psalm 34:18 (NIV)

Devotional

They scream. They stomp. They slam doors, roll eyes, argue, cry, yell, melt down — loudly and dramatically — in the middle of a grocery store, a family dinner, or your peaceful morning plan.

Sometimes it's a toddler in full tantrum mode. Sometimes it's a six-year-old who refuses to brush their teeth. Sometimes it's your teenager shutting you out, shouting something hurtful, or pushing back harder than you expected. And sometimes? It's you. Your voice that rises. Your chest that tightens. Your hands that shake. Your thoughts that spiral.

And in those moments — those messy, noisy, holy-hard moments — you feel like you're unraveling.

You try to stay calm. You try to breathe. You try to pray. But your prayers don't sound eloquent. They sound like, "Help." Like, "God, I don't know what to do." Like, "Please just get us through this."

And guess what? That prayer is enough.

The world tells you to "stay calm and carry on." But God says, *I'm with you — even here.* He doesn't need you to be composed. He just asks you to come.

The psalmist writes that the Lord is close to the brokenhearted — not just the grieving, but the emotionally exhausted. The moms who feel crushed under the weight of everyone else's emotions. The moms who feel helpless in the face of their child's storm.

In the chaos, God is not distant. He's close.

He's with you in the yelling, in the slammed doors, in the long silences that follow. In the part of you that wants to run away or scream into a pillow. He meets you in the pause — when you manage to stay still instead of snapping. He meets you in the aftermath — when you finally have space to cry.

And as impossible as it feels in the moment, these storms — theirs and yours — can become invitations. Invitations to grow in empathy. To show grace. To ask for forgiveness. To start over, again and again, with gentleness that only God can supply.

No meltdown lasts forever. And no emotional storm can cancel the love God has for you — or the love you're building into your child, moment by moment.

Prayer

God, I feel overwhelmed when emotions run high in our house. Sometimes I don't know how to help, and sometimes I'm part of the chaos. Please meet me in those moments. Teach me to pray through the storm and trust that You're present, even when I feel powerless. Amen.

Weave It Into Your Day

When tensions rise this week, pause and silently pray, "God, be near." Don't wait to feel calm — invite Him into the middle of it.

Week 26

WHEN THEY TALK BACK

SCRIPTURE

"A gentle answer turns away wrath, but a harsh word stirs up anger."

— Proverbs 15:1 (NIV)

Devotional

You ask a simple question, and the answer comes back laced with attitude. A sigh. An eye roll. A sarcastic comment or a tone that makes your whole body tense. You didn't mean to start a fight — you were just asking them to clean their room, or turn off the game, or answer a basic question without the drama. But suddenly, you're locked in a power struggle you didn't sign up for.

They're pushing buttons. Testing boundaries. Talking back. And everything in you wants to snap back with authority — louder, sharper, stronger — just to make it stop.

This is one of the hardest parts of motherhood: staying calm when someone you love deeply is coming at you with words that sting.

It's not just about disrespect. It's about what it stirs up inside of *you*. The fear that you're losing control. The frustration of being misunderstood. The exhaustion of always being the emotional anchor for everyone else.

But Proverbs gives us a simple — and challenging — reminder: "A gentle answer turns away wrath, but a harsh word stirs up anger." That's not just for your kids. It's for you, too.

Gentleness means strength under control. It means responding with wisdom when your emotions want to lead. And that's not something you do by yourself — it's something God *builds* in you over time.

This doesn't mean you ignore the disrespect or let your child speak to you however they want. Boundaries matter. Consequences teach. But how you deliver correction matters just as much as what you say.

Your tone can either escalate the tension or de-escalate it. Your response can either close a heart or open a door.

This doesn't mean you'll get it right every time. You're human. There will be days when you raise your voice, say something you regret, or walk away in frustration. But even those moments can become teaching moments — not just for your child, but for *you*.

Take time to cool down. Pray before you speak. Come back and model what it looks like to apologize when needed. That doesn't diminish your authority — it strengthens your relationship.

Talking back is part of their growing process. And learning to respond with grace is part of yours. God is shaping you both.

Prayer

Lord, I get so frustrated when I'm met with disrespect or defiance. I want to lead with wisdom, not emotion. Teach me to respond with gentleness and strength. Help me pause before I speak, and give me the words that build up, not break down. Help me grow patience and grace, even when it's hard. Amen.

Weave It Into Your Day

If you're met with a rude comment this week, pause. Take one breath. Then respond slower, softer, and more thoughtfully than you feel like. That one moment could change the whole tone.

Week 27

DISCIPLINING WITH LOVE

SCRIPTURE

"Those whom I love I rebuke and discipline. So be earnest and repent."

— Revelation 3:19 (NIV)

Devotional

Discipline is one of the most exhausting parts of parenting — not just because of what it demands from your child, but because of what it requires from *you*.

It's easy to give a consequence when you're angry. It's harder to follow through when you're calm. It's hard to correct behavior without wounding the heart. And it's even harder to strike the balance between being firm and being kind — especially when the same issue keeps coming up.

You don't want to be too harsh. You also don't want to be too passive. And on top of all that, you're trying to discipline while also managing your own exhaustion, frustration, and desire to just keep the peace.

But here's the good news: loving discipline isn't about getting it perfect. It's about staying connected while correcting.

God disciplines *because* He loves. His correction isn't rejection — it's redirection. He doesn't shame us, humiliate us, or lash out. He guides us with both truth and grace. And that's the model we're invited to follow.

It's okay to have rules. It's okay to set consequences. In fact, it's essential. Children feel safest when they know where the boundaries are. But how you enforce those boundaries can either build trust or tear it down.

Discipline should never be about power or control — it should be about connection and growth. Your goal isn't just to stop a behavior. It's to shape a heart. To help your child understand why something matters, not just that it's "wrong."

That takes time. It takes presence. And yes, it takes a whole lot of patience. But it also takes faith — faith that God is working through your consistency, your calm correction, your willingness to apologize when you mess up, and your refusal to shame your child when they do.

There's no one-size-fits-all approach to discipline. What works for one kid might backfire with another. What worked last year might not work this month. That's okay. You're learning as you go. So are they.

Keep showing up. Keep adjusting. Keep asking God to give you wisdom and tenderness in equal measure. And when you feel like you're failing, remind yourself: love isn't soft or strict — it's steadfast.

Prayer

God, I want to discipline with wisdom and love, but it's hard to know what's right in the moment. Help me not to react out of anger, but to respond with clarity and compassion. Give me the courage to set healthy boundaries, and the grace to lead with love, even when it's hard. Amen.

Weave It Into Your Day

Before correcting your child this week, pause and ask yourself: "What's the goal — control or connection?" Let that question guide your tone, your timing, and your words.

Week 28

FORGIVING FAST

SCRIPTURE

"Be kind and compassionate to one another, forgiving each other, just as in Christ God forgave you."

— Ephesians 4:32 (NIV)

Devotional

They said something hurtful. They rolled their eyes. They pushed your buttons, again. And while you tried to keep your cool, something inside you cracked — and now you're left holding a mixture of anger, sadness, and that nagging temptation to stay distant.

It's not that you don't love your child. You love them so much it hurts. But some moments leave bruises — little ones, maybe, but real ones. And forgiving them? Especially when it feels like they haven't really apologized or changed? That's hard. But it's also holy.

Forgiveness is one of the most Christlike things you'll ever do — and one of the most difficult. Especially when it comes to parenting. Because you're not just dealing with behavior. You're dealing with hearts — theirs and yours.

Forgiving doesn't mean ignoring the issue. It doesn't mean lack of consequences. And it certainly doesn't mean pretending it didn't hurt. It means: you don't let bitterness build a home in your heart.

Ephesians reminds us to forgive "just as in Christ God forgave you." That's the foundation —not their attitude, not their apology, not your emotions. *God's grace to you* empowers your grace to them.

And forgiveness is not just a gift for them — it's freedom for you. It softens the hard edges that build up after repeated tension. It restores the connection that gets frayed in the day-to-day. It lets you parent from love, not resentment.

Kids will mess up. So will you. That's part of the deal. But when forgiveness flows freely in your home — not just from parent to child, but from child to parent — you create a culture where grace is normal, not rare. That starts with you.

You go first — not because you always feel ready, but because love moves first. You say, "I forgive you," even when it's hard. You show your child that relationships are repaired through grace, not perfection.

And when *you* mess up, you model the other side of that same truth. You say, "I'm sorry," without defensiveness. You ask for forgiveness, and you show them that love can heal things that feel broken.

Forgiveness is a process. It takes practice. But when it becomes part of the rhythm of your home, it becomes part of your child's heart too.

Prayer

God, help me to forgive quickly. I don't want to carry resentment, especially with the people I love most. Teach me how to lead with grace, even when I've been hurt. Thank You for forgiving me, again and again. Help me pass that same gift on. Amen.

Weave It Into Your Day

Is there something lingering between you and your child? Take a deep breath, and choose to let it go. Say it aloud: "I forgive you." Then let love lead.

Week 29

WHEN YOU MISS WHO THEY WERE

SCRIPTURE

"There is a time for everything, and a season for every activity under the heavens."

— Ecclesiastes 3:1 (NIV)

Devotional

You see an old photo —the gap-toothed grin, the tiny shoes, the soft cheeks pressed against yours —and something inside you aches. It's not that you want to go back. But sometimes, you miss who they were.

You miss the way they used to curl up in your lap. The way they'd light up when you walked into the room. The questions that made you laugh. The chubby hands reaching for yours. The days when you were their whole world.

Now they barely fit in your arms. They're more independent, more opinionated. Maybe they roll their eyes more than they reach for your hand. Maybe you've traded bedtime snuggles for one-word answers. And even though you're proud of who they're becoming, part of you quietly mourns who they used to be.

This is one of the strange tensions of motherhood: holding deep joy for their growth alongside deep sadness that nothing stays the same.

Ecclesiastes tells us there is a time for everything — every season has its purpose. But God never says you have to breeze through changes with a smile. He made us emotional beings, so it's okay to feel tender as your child grows and changes.

It's okay to grieve the sweetness of past seasons. That doesn't mean you're ungrateful. It means you *loved well.* And anything deeply loved is also deeply missed when it changes.

But don't miss this: every season brings its own kind of beauty.

No, they may not run into your arms the way they used to. But maybe now they come to you with bigger questions — about friendship, identity, or faith. Maybe now your relationship is shifting into something richer, more complex, more reflective of the person they're becoming.

And the best part? You're still their safe place. Even when they act like they don't need you. Even when their affection looks different. You haven't lost your importance — your role is just evolving.

So go ahead and linger in that photo a little longer. Let the tears come if they need to. Then lift your eyes and look at the beautiful, growing child in front of you.

They're not who they were. But neither are you. You've both grown. And God is in this season, too.

Prayer

God, sometimes I miss the little version of my child. Help me hold space for those feelings without losing sight of the beauty in who they are becoming. Thank You for walking with us through every stage. Teach me to embrace the now — even when it's bittersweet — and to trust You with all the seasons ahead. Amen.

Weave It Into Your Day

Look at an old photo of your child today. Thank God for that season. Then say out loud, "And thank You for who they're becoming."

Week 30

MOM RAGE & MERCY

Scripture

"The Lord is compassionate and gracious, slow to anger, abounding in love."

— Psalm 103:8 (NIV)

Devotional

You didn't plan to yell. You were doing fine — or at least pretending to. But then something tipped you over. The mess that came right after you cleaned. The backtalk when you were just trying to help. The endless repetition of the same fight. And before you knew it, your voice was louder than you meant it to be. Your words, sharper. Your heart, pounding.

And now you're left with the aftermath — a slammed door, a quiet child, a pit in your stomach.

This is the part of motherhood no one likes to talk about. The rage that creeps in when you're overstimulated, overtired, overwhelmed. It's not just about anger — it's about the pressure that builds from always being "on." From holding everything together. From not having space to feel your own emotions while constantly managing everyone else's. You love your kids fiercely. But sometimes you feel like a shaken bottle — one bump away from bursting.

And then comes the guilt. The belief that "good moms" don't yell. That you've somehow undone all your love with one outburst. That you're the only one who struggles this way. But you're not the only one.

Psalm 103 reminds us of the nature of God: compassionate, gracious, *slow to anger*, abounding in love. That's not just a standard to live up to — it's a promise. Because this is the same God who sees *you* — not just as a mom, but as His daughter. When you snap, He doesn't recoil. He moves closer. He offers mercy. And He doesn't just offer it *to* you — He wants to grow it *in* you.

The rage isn't the end of the story. It can be a wake-up call. A signal that something deeper needs attention — rest, help, healing. And when you invite God into that space, real change becomes possible. Not perfection. But transformation.

Mercy begins when you stop pretending you don't struggle and start inviting God into the struggle itself.

So take a breath. Apologize when needed. Ask for forgiveness. Hug your child. And remember that love is not erased by a hard moment. It's proven by what comes next.

You are still a good mom. Not because you never lose it — but because you always come back with grace.

Prayer

God, I hate how I feel when I lose control. I don't want anger to lead the way in my parenting. Help me to pause, breathe, and turn to You when the pressure builds. Thank You for Your mercy — not just when I get it right, but especially when I don't. Grow Your compassion in me. Amen.

Weave It Into Your Day

If you lose your temper today, don't spiral. Step away, take a breath, and say, "God, help me start again — with mercy."

Week 31

IT'S OKAY TO NOT LOVE EVERY MOMENT

SCRIPTURE

"Rejoice in hope, be patient in affliction, be faithful in prayer."

— Romans 12:12 (NIV)

Devotional

There are moments in motherhood that feel like magic — tiny arms wrapped around your neck, laughter in the hallway, a spontaneous "I love you" that makes everything worth it. And then there are moments that feel the exact opposite...

Moments when no one listens. When attitudes are sharp and tension is high. When the mess is endless, your nerves are frayed, and your emotions are hovering somewhere between irritated and undone. When you fantasize about disappearing into the laundry room with chocolate and silence and not coming out until someone begs you with tears and snacks.

And in those moments, you might wonder: *Is it okay that I really, really don't like this right now?* Yes. It is.

You're allowed to not like the moment — even while loving your child. You're allowed to feel overwhelmed, stretched thin, disappointed, annoyed. Those feelings don't make you a bad mom. They make you human.

Romans 12:12 doesn't say, "Enjoy your affliction." It says, "Be patient in affliction." That means the hard moments are acknowledged, not ignored. And patience doesn't mean pretending everything's fine. It means staying grounded in faith while trusting that things won't always be this way.

There's no spiritual bonus for pretending you're okay when you're not. God isn't asking for your fake smile. He's asking for your honest heart.

Bring Him your frustration. Bring Him your boredom, your weariness, your quiet resentment that today is not what you hoped it would be. He can handle it. In fact, He wants it. Because that's where healing and perspective begin — not in pretending, but in pouring it all out before Him.

This moment may not be your favorite. You may not feel inspired, fulfilled, or particularly maternal. That's okay. Not every part of motherhood will feel joyful. But every part of it is sacred — not because it *feels* good, but because God meets you *in it*.

You don't have to force gratitude. You don't have to fake peace. You just have to stay open — open to grace, open to patience, open to the truth that this moment will pass, and God is still working through it.

Prayer

God, thank You for loving me even in the moments I don't love. Help me to be honest with You and with myself. I don't want to fake joy — I want to find it again, even if it takes time. Give me patience when the day feels long, and remind me that You are near, even in the moments I'd rather skip. Amen.

Weave It Into Your Day

If you find yourself not enjoying the moment today, pause. Say, "This is hard, but I'm not alone." Let that simple truth shift your heart, even slightly.

Week 32

CHOOSING LOVE OVER CONTROL

SCRIPTURE

"There is no fear in love. But perfect love drives out fear…"

— 1 John 4:18a (NIV)

Devotional

You want the best for them. You want them to be safe, healthy, kind, responsible, respectful, faith-filled. You want them to avoid heartache, bad decisions, and unnecessary pain. So you plan, teach, guide — and sometimes hover, overcorrect, or overreact.

Not because you don't trust them. Not even because you don't trust God. But because deep down, you're afraid: Afraid of what might happen if you don't step in; afraid of what they might become if you get it wrong; afraid of what the world might throw at them.

Fear makes you tighten your grip. But love invites you to let go.

This doesn't mean you stop parenting, setting boundaries, or being involved. It means you check your *motivation*. Are you correcting from fear, or leading from love? Are you trying to shape them with wisdom, or manage them with control?

It's a fine line — one that shifts from season to season. With toddlers, it's about managing behaviors. With older kids, it becomes more about influence than control. And eventually, parenting becomes less about holding on and more about *releasing with trust.*

That trust is not in your child's perfection. It's in God's presence with them — and with you.

1 John tells us that perfect love drives out fear. Not perfect parenting. Not perfect kids. *Perfect love.* That means love rooted in God — not in outcomes — has the power to calm your anxious heart. And when fear loosens its grip, love can take its rightful place.

Love that listens more than it lectures. Love that corrects without crushing. Love that respects their individuality while still guiding with intention. Love that says, "I'm here. I'm for you. I don't need to control you to be close to you."

It's okay to admit when control is creeping in. It's okay to ask God for help releasing your grip — on the outcome, the schedule, the grades, the choices, the timeline. Because your child's story doesn't rest entirely in your hands.

God loves them more than you do. And He's not panicked.

So breathe. You can lead with strength and tenderness. You can discipline with love instead of fear. You can trust that the same God who is parenting *you* is also walking with your child — even when you're not there to guide every step.

Prayer

God, I want to lead with love, but sometimes fear takes over. I try to control things because I care so deeply. Please help me release my grip and trust that You're at work in my child's life. Teach me to parent with courage, not anxiety — with wisdom, not control. Thank You for loving them even more than I do. Amen.

Weave It Into Your Day

Name one thing you've been trying to control. In prayer, release it to God. Say, "I choose love over fear. I choose trust over control."

PART FIVE

Strength for the Weary

Some days, you feel like you have nothing left to give. The demands are constant, the rest is scarce, and the weight of everything you carry feels too heavy to bear. You love your family deeply, but love doesn't erase exhaustion.

This section is for the weary days—the ones where you wonder if you're strong enough, patient enough, or even capable of doing this well. It's a reminder that *you don't have to be enough on your own.*

God never asked you to do it all. He never expected you to carry motherhood in your own strength. He offers rest—not just physical rest, but soul-deep renewal. He sees what no one else does. He fills in the gaps where you fall short. And when you feel like you can't get up again, He reminds you that grace is new every morning.

You don't have to run on empty. God is ready to fill you up.

Week 33

STRONGER THAN YOU THINK

Scripture

"But he said to me, 'My grace is sufficient for you, for my power is made perfect in weakness.' Therefore I will boast all the more gladly about my weaknesses, so that Christ's power may rest on me."

— 2 Corinthians 12:9 (NIV)

Devotional

You don't always feel strong. In fact, some days you feel anything but.

You feel tired from the moment you open your eyes. You juggle the demands of work, home, relationships, school forms, groceries, and emotional support like a circus act you never auditioned for. And most of the time, no one claps at the end.

You feel stretched thin — mentally, physically, emotionally. And still, you show up. You keep going. You pour out. You give again. You press through. Because love moves you forward, even when energy and confidence lag behind.

But on the inside? You question your strength. You wonder how long you can keep this up. And if one more thing falls apart, you might, too.

But here's the truth you need to remember: You are stronger than you think — not because you never break, but because you let God meet you in the breaking.

Strength in motherhood doesn't always look bold or loud. Sometimes it looks like whispering a prayer while picking up socks. Sometimes it looks like wiping tears — theirs or yours — and getting back up. Sometimes it's staying calm in the face of chaos. Other times, it's apologizing after you didn't.

You don't need to feel strong to *be* strong. God's Word tells us His power is made perfect in our weakness. Not in our hustle. Not in our illusion of control. But in our honest, trembling surrender.

You're not meant to do it all in your own strength. You were never expected to parent from a place of perfection. Your strength isn't measured by how much you carry — it's shown in your willingness to turn to God *with what you can't.*

And friend, look at what you've already made it through. Look at how many times you didn't think you could — but you did. Not because it was easy, but because grace held you. Because faith steadied you. Because love led you forward, one step at a time.

Don't let the weight of today convince you that you're weak. You are doing sacred work, and you are not alone. You are filled with the strength of the One who never runs out.

Prayer

Lord, I don't always feel strong. Sometimes I feel overwhelmed and unsure of how to keep going. Thank You that I don't have to be strong on my own. Your grace is enough. Help me to lean into Your strength and let go of the pressure to do it all myself. Remind me that my weakness is where You show up best. Amen.

Weave It Into Your Day

Look back on a time when you thought you wouldn't make it — but you did. Thank God for the quiet strength He gave you then. Let it remind you He'll do it again.

Week 34

DON'T DO IT ALL

SCRIPTURE

"Come to me, all you who are weary and burdened, and I will give you rest."

— Matthew 11:28 (NIV)

Devotional

There's a quiet pressure that hums beneath the surface of motherhood — the belief that if you don't do it all, everything might fall apart. So you do it all.

You stay up late to catch up on laundry. You volunteer even when your calendar is full. You remember every appointment, every lunch order, every birthday. You juggle logistics, emotions, and expectations like you were born for this.

And maybe you're good at it. Maybe no one even realizes how much you're holding — because you rarely drop anything.

But you feel it. In your body. In your spirit. In the moments when the to-do list wins and your joy starts to fade. In the whisper that wonders, *Is this just what motherhood is?*

God never asked you to do it all. He simply said, *Come to Me.*

Not when you're finished. Not once everything is under control. He invites you right in the middle of the overwhelm, offering rest where the world offers hustle.

Rest isn't weakness. It's wisdom. It's a holy recognition that you are not the center of everything — God is. And when you act like you have to carry it all, fix it all, and manage it all, you edge Him out of the very space He wants to fill.

Sometimes doing less is the most faithful thing you can do.

That doesn't mean you neglect what matters. It means you start asking different questions: What's mine to carry today? What can wait? What am I doing out of fear or guilt instead of calling?

You weren't meant to be everything to everyone. You were meant to live in rhythm with your Creator — work and rest, give and receive, pour out and fill up again. When you ignore that rhythm, you run dry. When you honor it, you live free.

It's okay to let the dishes wait. It's okay to say no to one more activity. It's okay to ask for help — and not feel guilty about it. You are allowed to rest. You are allowed to breathe. You are allowed to be a whole person, not just a production machine.

God didn't create you to do it all. He created you to walk with Him through it all — and trust that He's big enough to fill in the gaps.

Prayer

God, I'm tired of trying to do it all. I know You never asked me to carry everything by myself. Help me to release the pressure I've placed on myself. Teach me to trust You with what I can't do — and give me wisdom to know what truly matters. Thank You for offering rest when I need it most. Amen.

Weave It Into Your Day

Look at your to-do list for the day. Cross one thing off — not because it's done, but because it doesn't need to be done right now. Breathe in grace.

Week 35

WHAT REST REALLY LOOKS LIKE

SCRIPTURE

"In repentance and rest is your salvation, in quietness and trust is your strength..."

— Isaiah 30:15a (NIV)

Devotional

You try to rest, but even rest feels like a task.

You sit down — and your mind keeps spinning. You put your feet up —and you remember three things you forgot to do. You try to relax— but the guilt creeps in, telling you to be more productive.

And when you finally do get a moment "off," you scroll your phone, binge a show, or grab a snack — and somehow, you still feel tired afterward. That's because true rest isn't about stopping activity. It's about *receiving renewal.*

Rest isn't a nap (though those are holy too). It's not zoning out or numbing out. It's a posture of trust — of letting go of control and letting God be God. It's found in the quiet places where you remember that your worth isn't tied to your output, and your peace doesn't depend on your productivity.

In Isaiah, God speaks to His people with a countercultural invitation: "In repentance and rest is your salvation." Not in busyness. Not in proving yourself. In turning back to Him — and resting.

This isn't just about physical fatigue. It's about soul-weariness. That deep kind of tired you can't fix with a good night's sleep. The kind that comes from holding too much for too long. From caring deeply, loving fiercely, and managing more emotions than anyone knows.

You weren't designed to run nonstop. You were designed to live in rhythm — including sacred pauses. Rest is where your strength is restored. Where your identity is recalibrated. Where you stop hustling to be enough and remember that you *already are* — because God says so.

And here's the beautiful thing: rest doesn't have to be long or elaborate to be meaningful. It can be five minutes of silence in your car. A slow walk around the block. A whispered prayer while folding laundry. A few deep breaths with your eyes closed and your heart open.

Rest looks like saying no to one more thing — and not explaining why.

It looks like choosing presence over perfection.

It looks like trusting that the world will keep spinning — even if you pause.

You don't need to earn rest. You were made for it. And God, in His mercy, invites you into it again and again — not as a luxury, but as a lifeline.

Prayer

God, I'm tired. Not just in my body, but in my soul. Teach me what true rest looks like. Help me to let go of guilt, stop striving, and simply receive the peace You offer. Thank You for creating me with limits — and for meeting me in them with grace. Amen.

Weave It Into Your Day

Today, set a five-minute timer. Sit in stillness. Breathe slowly. Let God meet you in the quiet. Let rest be your act of trust.

Week 36

THE BEAUTY OF BORING DAYS

Scripture

"Give us today our daily bread."

— Matthew 6:11 (NIV)

Devotional

It's a regular day. The kind where nothing big happens. The laundry gets switched, dinner gets made, school pickups happen on time. There are no meltdowns, but no mountaintop moments either. Just ordinary.

And sometimes, that feels... underwhelming.

Motherhood is full of big feelings and constant movement, and the in-between days — the quiet ones — can start to feel like white noise. You wonder if you're doing anything meaningful, if these middle-of-the-road days matter at all, or if you're simply getting through them.

But boring days can be beautiful days.

They're the ones where faithfulness gets practiced in the unnoticed places. Where stability gets built without fanfare. Where the sacredness of routine offers something rare in a loud, fast world: peace.

In Matthew 6, Jesus taught His disciples to pray for daily bread. Not a week's worth. Not a lifetime supply. Just *today's* portion. It's a reminder that God meets us not only in the dramatic breakthroughs or deep valleys, but in the repetition of our daily lives.

These "boring" days are actually where most of life happens — and where much of love is proven.

When you pack the same lunch again. When you answer the same questions, fold the same clothes, show up for the same routines. These acts might feel small, but they are forming something powerful: consistency, safety, trust. Things your children might not even recognize now, but will feel the effects of for a lifetime.

And in the stillness of a day without drama, you have a rare opportunity to notice God more clearly — in the way the light hits the kitchen floor, in the sound of laughter two rooms away, in the silence that doesn't demand anything from you.

If you're constantly chasing significance in the form of excitement or emotional highs, you'll miss the holiness of the slow and steady. But if you can pause long enough to see what's *here*, you might just find beauty hiding in plain sight.

Because the God of miracles is also the God of Mondays. The God of ordinary chores and familiar rhythms. And He delights in meeting you not just in crisis or celebration, but in the calm.

Prayer

God, thank You for the quiet days. The uneventful ones. Help me not to overlook them or wish them away. Teach me to see Your hand in the ordinary — and to believe that these small acts of love and faithfulness matter deeply to You. Help me slow down enough to be present, even when the day feels plain. Amen.

Weave It Into Your Day

Today, notice one "boring" part of your routine — and thank God for it. Let it become a sacred space where you choose presence over distraction.

Week 37

ASKING FOR HELP ISN'T WEAK

SCRIPTURE

"Carry each other's burdens, and in this way you will fulfill the law of Christ."

— Galatians 6:2 (NIV)

Devotional

You've been holding a lot. Some of it is visible — schedules, chores, logistics. But some of it is silent — the mental load, the emotional labor, the worries you carry alone.

And maybe you've gotten really good at it. You know how to juggle the responsibilities. You know how to push through. People call you strong, dependable, amazing. But sometimes you wonder: *At what cost?*

You're tired. Not just physically, but deep-in-your-bones tired. And the thought of asking for help makes something inside you tense up. Because somewhere along the way, you may have picked up the lie that needing help means you're failing. That it's weakness. That it makes you less than. But Scripture tells a different story.

Galatians 6:2 says to carry one another's burdens. That's not just a nice suggestion — it's a reflection of Christ's love in action. God didn't design us to live in isolation, pretending we're fine. He created us for community — where needs are shared, not hidden. Where support flows in both directions. Where vulnerability makes room for grace. Asking for help isn't weak. It's wise. It's brave. It's holy.

You don't have to do everything yourself to prove your worth. You don't have to be the strong one all the time. Strength is not about how much you can carry alone — it's about knowing when to invite others in.

Maybe that means asking a friend to watch your kids. Maybe it means opening up to your partner about how overwhelmed you feel. Maybe it's reaching out to a counselor, a pastor, or a trusted friend and saying, "I'm not okay right now." You won't always be able to delegate the weight. But you *can* stop pretending it doesn't exist.

The people who love you don't want the polished version of you — they want the real you. And when you let them in, you give them permission to do the same. That's how authentic community is built. Not by impressing one another, but by supporting one another.

And when help comes? Receive it. With humility, with gratitude, without guilt. You're not a burden. Your needs are not an inconvenience. They're an opportunity — for connection, for compassion, for God to work through others in your life.

Prayer

God, it's hard for me to ask for help. I want to be strong, but sometimes I confuse independence with pride. Please teach me to invite others in — and to receive help with humility and grace. Remind me that I'm not meant to carry everything alone. Thank You for placing people in my life to walk with me. Amen.

Weave It Into Your Day

What's one thing you need help with right now? Name it. Then take one small step to ask — text a friend, delegate a task, or speak up. Let grace meet you there.

Week 38

WHEN NO ONE SEES

SCRIPTURE

"Your Father, who sees what is done in secret, will reward you."

— Matthew 6:4b (NIV)

Devotional

You do so much that no one sees. You refill the toilet paper roll. You remember the appointments. You know where everyone's favorite shirt is and how to decode their moods. You stay up late folding the laundry no one thanked you for, and you wake up early to get a head start no one notices.

You answer the hard questions, hold space for big feelings, smooth out the tension in conversations, and absorb the impact of everyone else's stress.

So much of motherhood happens in secret — behind doors, beneath the surface, outside the spotlight. And while you don't do it for applause, sometimes the lack of recognition stings. You wonder if it matters. If anyone notices. If the things you do day after day are even making a difference.

Let this be your reminder: **God sees it all.**

In Matthew 6, Jesus emphasizes the value of what's done in secret — not for show, not for validation, but out of love and faithfulness. And He promises that your Father, who sees it all, *will reward you.*

He honors what the world overlooks. He treasures the hidden sacrifices. He holds sacred the small, unseen acts of love that build your home from the inside out.

The carpool conversations. The prayers whispered over sleeping children. The extra grace you extend when you'd rather withdraw. The decision to start again, to show up again, to love again, even when you're exhausted — these are seeds being sown. And God is keeping track, even when no one else is.

You may never get public praise. You may not even get a "thank you" some days. But your faithfulness is not wasted. Heaven sees what your family might miss. And even when you feel invisible, you are never actually unseen.

God sees *you* — not just your output, but your heart. He sees your effort. Your longing. Your weariness. Your tears. He sees how hard you're trying, even when the day goes sideways. And He's not tallying your failures — He's walking with you in the middle of your faithfulness.

So don't minimize the work you're doing. It matters. It all matters. Not because it's big or flashy, but because it's done with love — and because it's seen by the One who matters most.

Prayer

God, sometimes I feel invisible. I do so much that no one notices, and I start to wonder if it really matters. Thank You for seeing what no one else sees — for honoring the quiet work of love and showing me that it is never wasted. Help me to serve with joy, knowing that I'm never alone or unseen. Amen.

Weave It Into Your Day

Choose one unseen act of service you do regularly. As you do it today, whisper: "God sees this." Let it remind you that your faithfulness is not forgotten.

Week 39

THE MIRACLE OF GETTING UP AGAIN

SCRIPTURE

"The steadfast love of the Lord never ceases; his mercies never come to an end; they are new every morning; great is your faithfulness."

— Lamentations 3:22–23 (ESV)

Devotional

Some days, you crush it. You wake up on time, the kids eat real food, you keep your cool, and maybe even check something off the list that's been haunting you for weeks.

Other days... not so much. You oversleep. You yell. You forget the permission slip. You question everything. And then comes the wave: *How am I supposed to do this again tomorrow?*

But here's the quiet miracle of motherhood — and of grace itself: **you get up again.**

You rise on weary legs. You pour cereal. You zip backpacks. You press forward into another day of showing up, even when you're carrying the weight of yesterday's discouragement. That is not failure. That is *faithfulness.*

God never said you had to be flawless. He said His mercies would be new — *every morning*. That means today's mess doesn't cancel tomorrow's mercy. It means every sunrise is another chance to start again, not because you earned it, but because He is faithful.

And getting up again isn't just about crawling out of bed. It's about returning to love. Returning to purpose. Returning to the quiet belief that, with God's help, you can keep going — even when it feels like you have nothing left.

You may not see it, but that choice — to keep going when no one's clapping, when nothing feels easy, when everything in you wants to stay down — is holy.

You're not expected to leap out of bed singing. But rising with intention — even if it's slow, even if it's messy — is a small act of resurrection.

Because every day, something in you is being renewed. Sometimes it's your patience. Sometimes it's your trust. Sometimes it's your ability to offer grace — to your kids *and* to yourself. That is the miracle.

The world celebrates flashy victories. God celebrates quiet resilience. The kind that gets up one more time than it fell down. The kind that doesn't wait to feel strong before stepping forward. The kind that leans on Him, moment by moment, breath by breath.

You don't have to do this perfectly. You just have to keep showing up. And when you can't? He'll meet you there too.

Prayer

God, thank You for new mercies every morning. Some days I feel like such a failure. But still, You invite me to begin again. Give me the strength to rise — not because I feel ready, but because You are with me. Thank You for the miracle of starting over. Amen.

Weave It Into Your Day

When you wake up tomorrow, pause before the day begins. Whisper this: "This is a new mercy. God, help me walk in it."

Week 40

GOD'S GOT THE GAPS

Scripture

"But he said to me, 'My grace is sufficient for you, for my power is made perfect in weakness.'..."

— 2 Corinthians 12:9 (NIV)

Devotional

You forgot to sign the form. You missed the tone in their voice that said they needed more from you. You lost your temper after promising yourself you'd stay calm. You meant to start that tradition... teach that lesson... show up better... be more present. But you didn't.

And now you feel the gap — that space between the mom you want to be and the mom you are. It feels wide. Sometimes it feels like everything important might fall into it. But here's the truth: God sees the gap — and He's already in it.

You were never meant to parent perfectly. You were meant to parent *faithfully*. Faithfulness isn't about flawless execution. It's about showing up again and again, even when you feel like you're falling short.

There will always be gaps — in your patience, your energy, your awareness, your consistency. But those gaps don't disqualify you. They create space for grace.

Paul wrote that God's power is made perfect in weakness. Not improved. Not covered up. *Perfected.* That means the very places where you feel most lacking might be the places where God's presence shines most brightly — not just in your life, but in your child's too.

God doesn't just work through your strengths. He works through your limitations. He works through the prayers you whisper in the hallway, the apologies you make through tears, the efforts no one sees but Him.

You can't control every influence, every outcome, every emotion. But you can trust the One who fills in the places you can't reach.

He's speaking to your child in ways you don't always see. He's shaping their heart in the quiet moments you don't remember. He's working behind the scenes, covering what you missed, healing what went sideways, redeeming what feels lost. That doesn't excuse us from growing or trying. But it frees us from carrying the impossible pressure of being everything, always.

You will mess up. You will overlook things. You will leave gaps. And still — God will meet you there. He's not asking you to be enough for your kids. He's asking you to trust that *He is.*

Prayer

God, thank You for covering the places where I fall short. I see all the ways I miss the mark, but You see all the ways You're still working. Help me let go of the guilt and lean into Your grace. I want to be faithful, not flawless. Teach me to trust You with the gaps. You are more than enough. Amen.

Weave It Into Your Day

Think of one area where you feel you're "not enough." Say it aloud, then follow it with this: "But God, You are." Let that truth carry you today.

PART SIX

Holy Moments

Not every day feels significant. Some moments feel too small to matter, too ordinary to be sacred. But motherhood is built on moments—the fleeting, often-overlooked spaces where love is formed and faith is quietly passed down.

This section is an invitation to see what's holy in the middle of what's normal. The bedtime prayers, the shared laughter, the simple joys, and even the unnoticed sacrifices—they all add up to something eternal.

God is in the now, not just the next. He is present in the whispered prayers, the silly giggles, the legacy being written one ordinary day at a time. And through every season, every shift, every change, one thing remains: *you are not just holding them—God is holding you, too.*

Week 41

DON'T MISS THE NOW

SCRIPTURE

"The Lord has done it this very day; let us rejoice today and be glad."

— Psalm 118:24 (NIV)

Devotional

There's always something coming next.

The next stage. The next milestone. The next appointment, meal, crisis, bedtime routine. And in the middle of it all, your mind races ahead — planning, bracing, anticipating.

You tell yourself: *Things will slow down soon. I'll enjoy them more when they're older. Next week will be better. After this season, I'll have time.* But if you're always chasing what's next, you risk missing what's now.

This day — not just the shiny, highlight-worthy parts, but the regular ones, too — is one God has acted in. He didn't just make it to be endured or checked off a list. He gave it to you to live — fully, intentionally, and with joy. Now matters.

The "now" might not be perfect. It might be chaotic or heavy or full of dishes and schoolwork and conflict. It might include a fussy toddler, a distant teenager, a frustrating middle school phase. It might feel like a holding pattern or a blur. But even this moment holds something sacred.

Because God is not only in your past or future — He's present. He's here. In the spilled juice. In the carpool. In the sticky hugs. In the eye rolls and late-night talks and scattered Legos. He's not waiting for you to "arrive" at a better season. He wants to meet you in *this* one.

And the beautiful — and heartbreaking — truth of motherhood is this: today won't last forever. The things that feel exhausting now might one day be the things you miss. The mess that makes you groan might hold the fingerprints of memories. The little phrases, the mispronounced words, the bedtime rituals — they're fleeting. And one day you'll think, *That was so ordinary. And it was so good.*

This isn't pressure to love every second. You don't have to force gratitude or pretend it's all magical. But if you can slow down just enough to *notice*, you might find beauty where you didn't expect it.

So put down the phone. Look your child in the eyes. Listen a little longer. Linger a little more. Don't rush through bedtime or brush off their questions. There's holiness in the ordinary — if you're willing to pause and see it.

The next thing will come. But for now, you're here. And that's enough.

Prayer

God, I move so fast. I'm always rushing to the next thing, the next task, the next phase. Help me slow down and really see what You've placed in front of me today. Teach me to find joy in the now — even when it's messy, even when it's hard — and to trust that You are here with me in it. Amen.

Weave It Into Your Day

Pause for 60 seconds today — and every day this week. Look around. Listen. Soak in the moment you're in — not the one coming next. Let it remind you: this is holy ground.

Week 42

BEDTIME IS SACRED

SCRIPTURE

"In peace I will lie down and sleep, for you alone, Lord, make me dwell in safety."

— Psalm 4:8 (NIV)

Devotional

Bedtime can be beautiful. It can also be bananas.

One child wants another drink. Another suddenly has a hundred deep thoughts. Someone forgot to brush their teeth, and someone else is melting down over a misplaced stuffed animal. And you? You're exhausted, counting the minutes until the house goes quiet.

But somewhere in the shuffle, bedtime often becomes a thin place — a quiet, holy stretch of time when hearts are softer, questions come more freely, and connection deepens, even after a hard day.

It's the moment when defenses drop. When your child, no matter their age, becomes just a little more tender. And in that moment, you're invited to do more than tuck in bodies — you get to speak peace over souls.

A whispered prayer. A forehead kiss. A reminder that they are loved, no matter what. These things matter. They echo. They become part of the rhythm that writes identity into your child's heart.

You won't always get it "right." Some nights you'll rush. Some nights there'll be tension or tears or too much noise. But over time, these small, repetitive rituals become sacred — not because they're perfect, but because they're *consistent.*

Bedtime says: "I see you." "You are safe." "You are loved, even after a rough day." "You don't have to earn rest — it's a gift."

And here's something else to remember: bedtime isn't just sacred for them. It's sacred for *you* too.

It's a moment to exhale. To release the day. To stop measuring your success by how much you got done or how patient you were. To breathe out the stress and breathe in grace.

Psalm 4:8 reminds us that we lie down in peace because God makes us dwell in safety. It's not our performance that secures rest — it's His presence. And that truth is for both of you.

So whether your bedtime routine includes storybooks or silence, long talks or quick hugs, let it become a sacred rhythm — a place where love is reaffirmed, grace is given, and God's peace wraps around you both.

Prayer

God, thank You for the gift of rest — not just physical rest, but emotional and spiritual peace. Help me to slow down at the end of the day and make space for connection. Let bedtime be more than a routine. Let it be a reminder of Your love, Your presence, and the safety You provide. Teach me to speak peace over my home, even in the chaos. Amen.

Weave It Into Your Day

This week, when you say goodnight, take 15 extra seconds. Speak one blessing — out loud or silently — over your child. Let bedtime be more than the end of a day. Let it be a beginning of peace.

Week 43

THE LEGACY YOU'RE LEAVING

SCRIPTURE

"But from everlasting to everlasting the Lord's love is with those who fear him, and his righteousness with their children's children."

— Psalm 103:17 (NIV)

Devotional

It's hard to think about legacy when you're picking Goldfish out of couch cushions and repeating yourself for the twentieth time before noon.

It feels like legacy belongs to big, sweeping gestures — founding charities, writing books, making history. But the truth is, most legacies are built in small moments. In repetition. In ordinary faithfulness no one claps for.

The legacy you're leaving isn't about one defining act. It's being defined every day — by the way you speak, the way you forgive, the way you show up again and again when no one's watching.

It's in the way you apologize after yelling. The way you let your child see you pray. The way you talk about people behind their backs (or don't). The way you comfort, correct, and carry on.

It's in the music playing in your home, the words written on sticky notes, the way you make space for feelings and teach your child that home is where they're loved — even when they're not at their best.

You are sowing seeds. Not every seed blooms right away. Some won't sprout until years from now. Some you may never see with your own eyes.

But every kind word, every boundary, every prayer whispered when they're asleep — it all adds up. These are the bricks in the foundation your child will stand on long after they've outgrown your lap.

Psalm 103 reminds us that God's love extends not only to us, but to our children's children. That's legacy. When your faithfulness ripples through generations, not because you were perfect, but because you pointed them toward the One who is.

Maybe your own legacy started with you — maybe you're breaking cycles, healing wounds, creating a different kind of home than the one you came from. That's holy work. And it matters more than you know.

You won't get everything right. No one does. But by living with intentionality and grace, by anchoring your home in love and inviting God into the middle of it, you are leaving something that will last.

Your child might not remember every detail of their childhood — but they'll remember how it *felt*. And that feeling? That's legacy.

Prayer

God, sometimes I feel like my days are too small to matter. But I trust that You're using the ordinary to build something eternal. Help me to be faithful with what's in front of me. Teach me to sow seeds of love, truth, and grace, even when I don't see the fruit right away. Let my legacy point my children toward You. Amen.

Weave It Into Your Day

Think of one value you hope to pass down. This week, live it out in a small way — speak it, model it, or pray it over your child. Let that quiet act shape tomorrow.

Week 44

A THANK YOU THEY MAY NEVER SAY

SCRIPTURE

"Whatever you do, work at it with all your heart, as working for the Lord, not for human masters."

— Colossians 3:23 (NIV)

Devotional

You packed the lunch. Again.

You remembered the permission slip. You kept calm when they rolled their eyes. You stayed up late washing the uniform, helping with the project, researching the weird rash. You gave them your last bite, your warmest blanket, your best energy — even when yours was gone. And most days? No one says, "Thank you."

Sometimes they forget. Sometimes they assume. Sometimes they're too young to notice or too old to realize. And sometimes, the gratitude just doesn't come — not in words, at least. And still, you give.

You pour yourself out in a hundred invisible ways. You serve in quiet places. You show up with faithfulness and love, again and again, even when no one acknowledges it. It's easy to feel unseen. To wonder if any of it matters. To ask, *Would they even notice if I stopped?*

But here's the truth: you're not just parenting for applause. You're parenting with purpose.

Colossians reminds us to work at everything with all our heart — not for the approval of others, but as an offering to God. That includes the parts of motherhood no one notices. The parts no one claps for. The parts that feel repetitive, thankless, and never-ending.

God sees every sacrifice. Every dish you wash. Every emotion you hold. Every bedtime story, every school run, every moment you choose love over frustration. He sees. He knows. And He's the one who says: *It matters.*

You may never get the thank-you you deserve — not in this season, maybe not ever. But your child is absorbing more than you know. One day, when they're packing their own lunches or comforting their own child, they may suddenly see it. Feel it. Understand it. And even if they never say the words, the legacy of your love will live on in how they care for others.

And besides — even if the world never sees, even if they never say thank you, *God already has.*

He's the one you're ultimately serving. And He promises that your quiet, faithful love is never wasted.

Prayer

God, sometimes I feel invisible. I give so much without thanks or recognition, and it's hard not to let resentment creep in. Remind me that You see it all — every small act of love, every tired yes, every quiet sacrifice. Help me to serve with joy, not for applause, but for You. Let my faithfulness reflect Your love, even when no one else notices. Amen.

Weave It Into Your Day

Think of one "thankless" thing you do often. As you do it this week, say: "God, I do this for You." Let that shift your perspective — from unnoticed chore to holy offering.

Week 45

THESE ARE THE GOOD OLD DAYS

SCRIPTURE

"Teach us to number our days, that we may gain a heart of wisdom."

— Psalm 90:12 (NIV)

Devotional

You scroll through old photos and feel it — that ache of time moving too fast. The baby cheeks. The squeaky voices. The tiny shoes you swore you just bought, now outgrown and forgotten at the back of the closet.

And you wonder: *Were those the good old days? Did I notice them while they were happening?*

But what if you're in them now? Right here — in the crumbs under the table, the backpacks on the floor, the texts about forgotten homework, the bedtime stalling — this could be the season you look back on with misty eyes and full heart. The one you'll tell stories about. The one that shaped them... and you.

It doesn't always feel magical. Some days feel like a grind. You're tired. You're stretched. You're wondering if you're making any progress or just running in circles. But often, the seasons that feel like "too much" in the moment are the ones we remember with the most fondness later.

Not because they were easy — but because they were *full*.

Psalm 90 reminds us to number our days — not just count them, but pay attention to them. To recognize their value while we're still living them. To gain wisdom by slowing down enough to see what's sacred in the middle of the messy.

You won't savor every moment. Some are too loud, too hard, too draining. But every once in a while, pause and look around. Soak it in — the way their hair falls in their eyes, the way they still call you "Mommy," the chaos that somehow makes your house feel alive.

This isn't about pretending things are perfect. It's about resisting the lie that joy is always later — when things calm down, when they're more independent, when you're more rested.

Joy is *now*.

Right here in the middle of real life. Right here in the spilled milk, the belly laughs, the car ride conversations, the mess that means people are living and growing under your roof.

One day, you might miss this version of your life. So be here for it.

Not every second. Not with constant gratitude. But with enough awareness to say, *This might be harder than I expected — and more beautiful than I realized.*

Prayer

God, help me not to miss what You're doing right now. I don't want to sleepwalk through these days, always waiting for the next season. Teach me to number my days — to find joy in the ordinary and beauty in the chaos. Let me see today not just as something to survive, but as a gift to treasure. Amen.

Weave It Into Your Day

Pause. Take a mental snapshot. Say out loud, "This is part of the good old days." Let it settle into your soul.

Week 46

GOD IN THE GIGGLES

SCRIPTURE

"A cheerful heart is good medicine..."

— Proverbs 17:22a (NIV)

Devotional

There's a sound that cuts through the chaos — unexpected and pure. Laughter.

The kind that bubbles up without planning. The kind that fills a room and shifts the atmosphere. The kind that makes your tired heart pause and remember: *Oh right. This is joy.*

Motherhood is full of intensity — of structure, logistics, emotions, and the never-ending hum of responsibility. But in between the tasks and tantrums and to-do lists, there are these little bursts of holy lightness: giggles.

A mispronounced word. A silly face. A dance party in the kitchen. A shared inside joke. A baby's belly laugh. A teen's rare smirk that turns into something real.

And if you're paying attention — really paying attention — you'll see God in it. Because joy isn't a distraction from the sacred. It *is* sacred.

We sometimes treat laughter like an extra — something to enjoy when the work is done, when things are going well, when the house is clean and the stress is low. But Proverbs tells us a cheerful heart is good medicine. That means it's not just optional — it's healing.

Laughter resets the room. It softens tension. It reconnects hearts. And in a season of life that can feel so heavy, these moments of lightness are not to be brushed aside. They're part of what sustains you.

Joy doesn't mean everything is easy. It means you found a reason to smile in the middle of everything that isn't.

Let yourself laugh. Let yourself be silly. Let yourself enjoy the moment without needing to document it or make it productive.

And let your kids see that side of you — not just the manager, the enforcer, the planner — but the one who can laugh until she cries. The one who sings the wrong lyrics, makes up bedtime stories, and knows how to find delight in the middle of an ordinary Tuesday.

God is not only present in quiet prayers and deep conversations. He is also present in joy. In silliness. In spontaneous dance breaks. In the sound of your child laughing — and the sound of you laughing with them.

These giggles are more than background noise. They're signs of life, signs of love, signs of God at work in the rhythm of your home.

Prayer

God, thank You for laughter — for the way it lifts the heaviness and reminds me of the beauty in everyday moments. Help me not to overlook the joy in front of me. Give me eyes to see You in the giggles, the silliness, and the smiles. Let laughter be part of the worship in our home. Amen.

Weave It Into Your Day

Find a way to be playful this week. Tell a joke. Make a funny face. Join in the laughter. Let joy break through, and let yourself enjoy it fully.

Week 47

SEEDS AND SEASONS

SCRIPTURE

"Let us not become weary in doing good, for at the proper time we will reap a harvest if we do not give up."

— Galatians 6:9 (NIV)

Devotional

Parenting can feel like planting seeds in a windstorm.

You pour in love, wisdom, truth, correction, patience, and more snacks than you can count — but some days it feels like nothing is growing. Like all the work, all the repetition, all the prayers are falling into the dirt and disappearing.

You want to see fruit. You want the attitude to shift, the lesson to stick, the bedtime routine to actually work. You want proof that what you're doing matters. But seeds don't sprout on demand. And growth is almost always invisible at first.

Galatians 6:9 reminds us not to grow weary in doing good — not because it will feel rewarding right away, but because there *will* be a harvest. *In due time.* Not necessarily on your timeline. But in God's.

That means your job isn't to control the outcome. It's to keep planting. Keep planting kindness. Keep planting truth. Keep planting the habit of prayer and the rhythm of grace. Keep showing up when it would be easier to check out. Keep loving when the return feels minimal.

You're not failing if it feels slow. You're not failing if you don't see fruit yet. Growth takes time. Seasons are long. And the harvest is God's responsibility — not yours.

Every time you respond with gentleness instead of snapping — seed. Every time you take a breath before correcting — seed. Every time you choose presence over perfection — seed. Every time you ask for forgiveness, offer mercy, or remind them they're loved — seed.

Some will take root right away. Some will sprout when they're older. Some may bloom in ways you never expected. But nothing planted in love is wasted in God's hands.

And just as your child is growing, so are you. The work you're doing in them is also being done *in you*. Your patience, your faith, your capacity to love — all of it is deepening, maturing, bearing fruit of its own. You don't have to rush the season. You just have to be faithful in it.

Keep planting. Keep watering. Keep trusting that God is doing what only He can do beneath the surface.

Prayer

God, sometimes I feel discouraged when I don't see progress. I want to know that what I'm doing matters. Remind me that seeds grow slowly — and that You are faithful to bring the harvest. Help me keep showing up, keep loving well, and keep planting truth, even when I don't see results right away. Thank You for doing the deep work in me and my child. Amen.

Weave It Into Your Day

Think of one "seed" you've planted in your child — a value, a habit, a prayer. Thank God for the unseen work happening beneath the surface. Trust Him with the harvest.

Week 48

HE'S HOLDING YOU, TOO

SCRIPTURE

"He tends his flock like a shepherd: He gathers the lambs in his arms and carries them close to his heart; he gently leads those that have young."

— Isaiah 40:11 (NIV)

Devotional

You spend most of your day holding someone or something.

A child on your hip. A laundry basket. A backpack. A to-do list in your mind. You hold shoes and snacks and schedules. You hold space for meltdowns and big feelings. You hold things together when it feels like everything's coming apart.

But somewhere in the middle of all that holding, you may forget that *you* are being held, too.

Isaiah 40:11 gives us a picture of a God who is not distant or detached. He doesn't just assign strength and send you on your way. He gathers you in His arms. He carries you close to His heart. He *gently leads* those with young — not with pressure, but with tenderness.

And that moment — when you stop just long enough to remember that — is sacred.

Because being held by God in the midst of motherhood isn't just comforting. It's holy. It's one of those quiet, fleeting reminders that grace is already present, even in the parts of your day that feel chaotic or unspiritual or too loud to hear from heaven.

Maybe you think of holy moments as candlelit prayers, whispered Scriptures, or serene stillness. But sometimes, holiness shows up in the most exhausted places — in the sigh you let out while folding laundry, in the way your voice softens even after a long day, in the exhale of surrender when you say, *"God, I can't do this without You."*

Those are the moments He carries you.

And here's the truth: you don't have to be strong every moment of every day. You don't have to hold it all together on your own. It's okay to feel weak, stretched thin, undone. That's not failure — it's the opening where grace pours in.

You carry so much — but you are carried, too.

And even when you don't feel it, God is holding you close.

So the next time your hands are full and your heart feels heavy, take a second to pause. That moment? It might be the most sacred one of your day.

Prayer

God, sometimes I forget that I'm allowed to lean on You. I carry so much for others that I don't always make space to receive Your care. Thank You for gently leading me, for holding me close, and for reminding me that I don't have to do it all. Help me to see Your presence in the ordinary and to rest in the holy moment of being held. Amen.

Weave It Into Your Day

Take one moment today — even thirty seconds — to pause and whisper, "God, thank You for holding me." Let that quiet truth follow you into the mess and the beauty.

PART SEVEN
Final Reflections

Motherhood is a journey—not just for your children, but for you.

Every sleepless night, every hard conversation, every moment of grace and growth is shaping you just as much as it's shaping them. You are not the same person you were when this journey began, and you won't be the same person a year from now. That's a good thing.

This final section is a reminder that faithfulness is found in the quiet, unseen moments. That the messiness of motherhood doesn't make it less holy—it makes it real. And that no matter how chaotic, imperfect, or overwhelming it gets, you are **still sacred, still seen, and still deeply loved** by the God who walks with you through it all.

You're not just raising them. *God is raising you, too.*

Week 49

YOU'RE STILL BECOMING

SCRIPTURE

"Being confident of this, that he who began a good work in you will carry it on to completion until the day of Christ Jesus."

— Philippians 1:6 (NIV)

Devotional

You spend so much time watching your children grow — charting their height, noticing their emotional shifts, marveling at how quickly they change — that it's easy to forget something important: You're still growing, too.

Just because you're the adult doesn't mean you've arrived. Just because you're the one doing the teaching doesn't mean you're finished learning. Motherhood doesn't freeze you in place — it *shapes* you. Day by day. Challenge by challenge. Grace by grace.

You're still becoming. God is not done with you just because you're in charge of little people now. He's still writing your story, still maturing your faith, still refining your character — not in spite of motherhood, but *through it.*

You may not always recognize it, because your growth isn't marked by milestones or measured in inches. It shows up in smaller, quieter ways — in the patience you didn't used to have. In the way you pause before reacting. In the tenderness that emerges from your own moments of failure. In the courage it takes to apologize, try again, and ask for help.

Philippians 1:6 reminds us that the good work God started in us is still underway. That means who you were when this parenting journey began is not who you are now — and it's not who you'll be a year from now, either. There's beauty in that.

You're not just raising a child. You're being raised, too — into someone softer, stronger, wiser, and more dependent on God than ever before.

So when you feel like you're still figuring it out? You are. When you realize you could've handled something better? That's growth. When you look back and cringe at how you used to respond? That's grace.

You don't need to be fully formed to be faithful. You just need to keep showing up. To keep learning. To keep letting God mold you in the middle of the mess.

Motherhood doesn't stall your spiritual growth — it accelerates it. It brings your flaws to the surface so God can heal them. It exposes your limits so He can expand your strength. It invites you to lean on Him more deeply than ever before. You're not behind. You're becoming.

Prayer

God, thank You for reminding me that I'm still in process. I don't have to have it all figured out to be faithful. Help me grow through this season. Use motherhood not just to shape my child, but to shape *me*. Help me see my own becoming as part of Your good work. Amen.

Weave It Into Your Day

Think back to who you were five years ago. What has changed? What has softened? Thank God for the quiet transformation still unfolding in you.

Week 50

THE QUIET KIND OF FAITHFULNESS

SCRIPTURE

"Let us hold unswervingly to the hope we profess, for he who promised is faithful."

— Hebrews 10:23 (NIV)

Devotional

Some days feel holy. Others just feel... repetitive.

You pack the lunch again. You answer the same questions, wipe the same counters, remind them to be kind, to brush their teeth, to stop fighting, to please just put their shoes on. Again.

There are no big wins, no dramatic revelations — just ordinary, necessary tasks strung together in a blur. And in the quiet monotony of it all, you start to wonder: *Is this really faithfulness? Or just survival?*

But faithfulness doesn't always look loud. It doesn't always feel inspiring. Often, it looks like showing up — again and again — with love and intention, even when no one's watching. Even when it's thankless. Even when you're not sure it's working.

It looks like choosing presence over perfection; pausing to pray before reacting; trying again when yesterday was hard. It looks like honoring your role — not because it's glamorous, but because it's *good*.

Faithfulness is what turns routines into rhythms of love. It's what builds trust, stability, and safety over time. It's what teaches your child that love doesn't depend on mood or convenience — it's steady. Consistent. There. And the world may never applaud your faithfulness, but heaven notices.

Hebrews 10:23 reminds us to hold unswervingly to the hope we profess — *because God is faithful.* That means your faithfulness is not just about willpower. It's about mirroring the God who shows up for you every single day. The God who never leaves. The God who honors the small and the unseen. Every ordinary act of motherhood is an echo of His love.

You may not get everything right. You may not feel holy. But when you love with patience, lead with grace, and keep going even when it's hard — that's sacred ground.

And here's the beautiful truth: your child is learning what faithfulness looks like by watching you. They're learning that love sticks around. That care is expressed in repetition. That God's presence is steady and sure — just like yours. You don't have to be extraordinary. You just have to be faithful.

Prayer

God, some days feel so ordinary that I wonder if they even matter. But I know You see every small act of love, every quiet "yes," every moment I choose to show up again. Thank You for being faithful to me. Help me reflect that same faithfulness to my family. Teach me to see holiness in the repetition — and joy in the quiet work of love. Amen.

Weave It Into Your Day

As you go through the day's routine, pause during one small task and say, "This is faithfulness." Let that reframe how you see your day — not as mundane, but as meaningful.

Week 51

MESSY, BUT HOLY

SCRIPTURE

"Do not despise these small beginnings, for the Lord rejoices to see the work begin..."

— Zechariah 4:10a (NLT)

Devotional

There are days when it all just feels... messy.

The living room is messy. The schedule is messy. Your emotions are messy. The conversations, the laundry pile, the way you reacted to that one thing you promised yourself you'd handle better — all of it.

And in the middle of it, you wonder: *How could this possibly be holy?*

We tend to think of holiness as neat, calm, reverent. But if you look closely at Scripture, God shows up in the mess all the time — in stables and storms, wildernesses and weeping. He's not afraid of disorder. He doesn't withdraw when things get chaotic. In fact, those are often the places He draws *nearest.*

Motherhood is not tidy. It's not linear. It's full of interruptions, unpredictability, and imperfections — yours and theirs. But that doesn't make it less sacred. It makes it more real.

Holiness isn't about looking perfect. It's about choosing love in the middle of the mess. It's about getting low to comfort a crying child. Pausing to breathe instead of yelling. Making peanut butter sandwiches for the fifth time this week. Wiping tears — theirs and your own — and whispering a prayer for strength. These aren't distractions from the spiritual life. *They are the spiritual life.*

God rejoices in the work you're doing — not just the polished parts, but the honest, messy, in-process ones. Zechariah 4:10 tells us not to despise small beginnings. Why? Because God *rejoices* in seeing the work begin.

That means He celebrates your attempts. Your try-agains. Your "I'm sorry"s. Your willingness to keep going. He sees the holy undercurrent running through your ordinary, imperfect days.

And maybe that's the invitation: to stop waiting for things to feel peaceful in order to believe God is present — and start believing that He's already here, in the pile of Legos and the scattered shoes and the awkward silence after an argument.

This is holy ground. Not because it looks beautiful — but because love lives here. Forgiveness lives here. Growth lives here. And so does God.

Prayer

God, some days feel so far from holy. The mess, the noise, the unfinished tasks, the imperfect moments — they all feel too small or too flawed to matter. But You are present even here. Help me see the sacredness in the everyday. Remind me that You rejoice not in my perfection, but in my faithfulness. Make this messy, ordinary life a place where Your love can be seen. Amen.

Weave It Into Your Day

Look around your space — the mess, the clutter, the signs of life. Whisper, "This is holy, too." Let it shift how you see what's around you... and what's within you.

Week 52

STILL SACRED, STILL LOVED

SCRIPTURE

"For I am convinced that neither death nor life, neither angels nor demons, neither the present nor the future... nor anything else in all creation, will be able to separate us from the love of God."

— Romans 8:38–39 (NIV)

Devotional

You've made it through a year of ups and downs, joy and exhaustion, laughter and tears. You've read words that reminded you of God's presence, even in the middle of spilled cereal, burned pancakes, teenage silence, and sleepless nights.

And here you are — still standing, still mothering, still becoming.

But maybe today, you don't feel especially spiritual. Maybe you feel behind. Worn thin. Still struggling with the same patterns. Still wondering if what you're doing is enough. Still carrying guilt, worry, or the weight of your own expectations.

Here's the truth: You are still sacred. Still loved.

God's love for you isn't fragile. It doesn't rise and fall with your performance. It doesn't depend on how patient you were this week or how much laundry you conquered. It is *steadfast*. Unshakeable. Constant through every high and low.

Romans 8 reminds us there is nothing that can separate us from the love of God. Not your failures. Not your doubts. Not your rough days. Not even your distance.

You are His — on the days you feel full of faith and on the days you feel like you're barely holding it together.

This journey you're on? It's holy. Not because it's always peaceful or beautiful or picture-perfect, but because **God is in it with you**. He walks with you through the chaos. He whispers truth in the mundane. He strengthens you in the weariness. He cheers for you when you rise again after falling.

You don't graduate from needing His grace. And you never outgrow His love.

So as this year comes to a close — whether you've read every word or skipped a few along the way — take a moment to rest in this simple but powerful reminder:

You are still sacred.

Still seen.

Still chosen.

Still held.

Still loved.

Not because you've done everything right, but because He is the God who meets you in the middle of it all — the One who doesn't just call you to mother well, but who mothers *you* with compassion, mercy, and unfailing love.

Prayer

God, thank You for carrying me through this year. For showing up in ways I didn't expect and for holding me through the hard and beautiful parts of motherhood. Help me believe that I am still sacred, even when life feels messy. Still loved, even when I feel like I'm not enough. May I continue to walk in Your grace, knowing You are always with me. Amen.

Weave It Into Your Day

Take a quiet moment today. Put your hand over your heart. Breathe deeply. Whisper, "I am still sacred. I am still loved." Let it be your benediction — and your beginning.

Before You Go...

You've made it to the end of this book—but not the end of this journey. Motherhood keeps unfolding, one day at a time, and so do you.

Maybe you read this devotional in order, maybe you jumped around, maybe you picked it up in moments of desperation or exhaustion. However you made your way through these pages, I hope you walk away with this truth planted deep in your heart:

Your faithfulness matters. Even when it feels small. Even when it goes unseen. Even when you question whether you're doing enough.

The work of mothering—wiping tears, setting boundaries, making meals, whispering prayers—*is sacred.* It may not always feel significant, but God sees every quiet act of love. And beyond that, He sees *you.*

You are not just raising children. You are growing, too.

The same God who walks with your child is walking with you. Through every season, through every late-night worry and early-morning sigh, through every moment you wonder if you have what it takes—**He is there.**

And the good news? **You don't have to be perfect to be faithful.**

There will still be hard days. You'll still have moments where you lose your patience, question your decisions, or feel like you're barely keeping up. But you are not meant to do this in your own strength. God's grace is new every morning. And He will keep filling in the gaps, guiding your steps, and holding you through it all.

So keep going, mama. **Not perfectly, but faithfully.**

And as you do, may you remember this:

- You are doing holy work, even when it feels ordinary.
- You are deeply loved, even on the days you feel unworthy.
- You are never alone—God is with you, in every moment, in every mess, in every step forward.

A Final Blessing

May you walk in grace, knowing that your love is enough.

May you find joy in the ordinary and peace in the chaos.

May you always remember that you are deeply seen, deeply loved, and never alone.

This is sacred work. And you are sacred, too.

Did you enjoy this book?

If it encouraged you, made you feel seen, or helped you draw closer to God in the middle of your messy, beautiful life—would you take a moment to leave a review?

Your words can help other moms discover *Sacred Chaos* and find the same hope and grace you did. Just a few words can make all the difference in the world!

Just scan or click (of ebook only) the QR code below, or go back to your orders page on Amazon:

If you would like another copy of this book, just click or scan this:

Thank you in advance for sharing the journey.

David & Mary Beth

* * *

OTHER BOOKS BY DAVID & MARY BETH:

Faith in Action -- Devotional for Teen Boys: A 52-Week Guide to Strengthen Faith, Build Character, Follow His Path, and Live with Purpose Through the Bible and Prayer

Faith and Wisdom -- Devotional for Teen Girls: A 52-Week Guide to Deepen Faith, Build Wisdom, Trust His Plan, and Live with Grace Through the Bible and Prayer